Q - 41

ISBN 0-8373-7041-8

TEST YOUR KNOWLEDGE SERIES

WHAT DO *You* KNOW ABOUT...
Diesel Engine Repair

QUESTIONS AND ANSWERS

D1611565

Test Your Knowledge In Your Area Of Interest Or Study By Giving Yourself Complete Exams! Then Grade Yourself.

- Discover Areas Of Strength And Weakness.
- Improve Test Scores.

2-94

#29868154

NLC
NATIONAL LEARNING CORPORATION

Copyright © 1991 by

National Learning Corporation

212 Michael Drive, Syosset, New York 11791
(516) 921-8888

PRINTED IN THE UNITED STATES OF AMERICA

PASSBOOK®
NOTICE

PASSBOOK SERIES®

The *PASSBOOK SERIES*® has been created to prepare applicants and candidates for the ultimate academic battlefield — the examination room.

At some time in our lives, each and every one of us may be required to take an examination — for validation, matriculation, admission, qualification, registration, certification, or licensure.

Based on the assumption that every applicant or candidate has met the basic formal educational standards, has taken the required number of courses, and read the necessary texts, the *PASSBOOK SERIES*® furnishes the one special preparation which may assure passing with confidence, instead of failing with insecurity. **Examination questions —** together with answers — are furnished as the basic vehicle for study so that the mysteries of the examination and its compounding difficulties may be eliminated or diminished by a sure method.

This book is meant to help you pass your examination provided that you qualify and are serious in your objective.

The entire field is reviewed through the huge store of content information which is succinctly presented through a provocative and challenging approach — the question-and-answer method.

A climate of success is established by furnishing the correct answers at the end of each test.

You soon learn to recognize types of questions, forms of questions, and patterns of questioning. You may even begin to anticipate expected outcomes.

You perceive that many questions are repeated or adapted so that you gain acute insights, which may enable you to score many sure points.

You learn how to confront new questions, or types of questions, and to attack them confidently and work out the correct answers.

You note objectives and emphases, and recognize pitfalls and dangers, so that you may make positive educational adjustments.

Moreover, you are kept fully informed in relation to new concepts, methods, practices, and directions in the field.

You discover that you are actually taking the examination all the time: you are preparing for the examination by "taking" an examination, not by reading extraneous and/or supererogatory textbooks.

In short, this PASSBOOK,® used directedly, should be an important factor in helping you to pass your test.

BASIC FUNDAMENTALS OF ENGINES, FUELS, LUBRICANTS, AND POLLUTION CONTROL

CONTENTS

DIESEL ENGINES

TROUBLE SHOOTING

CONTENTS

HOW TO TAKE A TEST

You have studied hard, long, and conscientiously.

With your official admission card in hand, and your heart pounding, you have been admitted to the examination room.

You note that there are several hundred other applicants in the examination room waiting to take the same test.

They all appear to be equally well prepared.

You know that nothing but your best effort will suffice. The "moment of truth" is at hand: you now have to demonstrate objectively, in writing, your knowledge of content and your understanding of subject matter.

You are fighting the most important battle of your life -- to pass and/or score high on an examination which will determine your career and provide the economic basis for your livelihood.

What extra, special things should you know and should you do in taking the examination?

BEFORE THE TEST

YOUR PHYSICAL CONDITION IS IMPORTANT

If you are not well, you can't do your best work on tests. If you are half asleep, you can't do your best either. Here are some tips:
1. Get about the same amount of sleep you usually get. Don't stay up all night before the test, either partying or worrying -- DON'T DO IT.
2. If you wear glasses, be sure to wear them when you go to take the test. This goes for hearing aids, too.
3. If you have any physical problems that may keep you from doing your best, be sure to tell the person giving the test. If you are sick or in poor health, you really cannot do your best on any test. You can always come back and take the test some other time.

AT THE TEST

EXAMINATION TECHNIQUES

1. Read the *general* instructions carefully. These are usually printed on the first page of the examination booklet. As a rule, these instructions refer to the timing of the examination; the fact that you should not start work until the signal and must stop work at a signal, etc. If there are any *special* instructions, such as a choice of questions to be answered, make sure that you note this instruction carefully.

1

2. When you are ready to start work on the examination, that is as soon as the signal has been given, read the instructions to each question booklet, underline any key words or phrases, such as *least, best, outline, describe*, and the like. In this way you will tend to answer as requested rather than discover on reviewing your paper that you *listed without describing*, that you selected the *worst* choice rather than the *best* choice, etc.

3. If the examination is of the objective or so-called multiple-choice type, that is, each question will also give a series of possible answers: A,B,C, or D, and you are called upon to select the best answer and write the letter next to that answer on your answer paper, it is advisable to start answering each question in turn. There may be anywhere from 50 to 100 such questions in the three or four hours allotted and you can see how much time would be taken if you read through all the questions before beginning to answer any. Furthermore, if you come across a question or a group of questions which you know would be difficult to answer, it would undoubtedly affect your handling of all the other questions.

4. If the examination is of the essay-type and contains but a few questions, it is a moot point as to whether you should read all the questions before starting to answer any one. Of course if you are given a choice, say five out of seven and the like, then it is essential to read all the questions so you can eliminate the two which are most difficult. If, however, you are asked to answer all the questions, there may be danger in trying to answer the easiest one first because you may find that you will spend too much time on it. The best technique is to answer the first question, then proceed to the second, etc.

5. Time your answers. Before the examination begins, write down the time it started, then add the time allowed for the examination and write down the time it must be completed, then divide the time available somewhat as follows:
   a. If 3 1/2 hours are allowed, that would be 210 minutes. If you have 80 objective-type questions, that would be an average of about 2 1/2 minutes per question. Allow yourself no more than 2 minutes per question, or a total of 160 minutes, which will permit about 50 minutes to review.
   b. If for the time allotment of 210 minutes, there are 7 essay questions to answer, that would average about 30 minutes a question. Give yourself only 25 minutes per question so that you have about 35 minutes to review.

6. The most important instruction is *to read each question* and make sure you know what is wanted. The second most important instruction is to *time yourself properly* so that you answer every question. The third most important instruction is to *answer every question*. Guess if you have to but include something for each question. Remember that you will receive no credit for a blank and will probably receive some credit if you write something in answer to an essay question. If you guess a letter, say "B" for a multiple-choice question, you may have guessed right. If you leave a blank as the answer to a multiple-choice question, the examiners may respect your feelings but it will not add a point to your score.

7. Suggestions

   a. Objective-Type Questions

     (1) Examine the question booklet for proper sequence of pages and questions.

     (2) Read all instructions carefully.

     (3) Skip any question which seems too difficult; return to it after all other questions have been answered.

     (4) Apportion your time properly; do not spend too much time on any single question or group of questions.

     (5) Note and underline key words -- *all, most, fewest, least, best, worst, same, opposite*.

     (6) Pay particular attention to negatives.

     (7) Note unusual option, e.g., unduly long, short, complex, different or similar in content to the body of the question.

     (8) Observe the use of "hedging" words - *probably, may, most likely, etc.*

     (9) Make sure that your answer is put next to the same number as the question.

     10) Do not second guess unless you have good reason to believe the second answer is definitely more correct.

    (11) Cross out original answer if you decide another answer is more accurate; do not erase.

    (12) Answer all questions; guess unless instructed otherwise.

    (13) Leave time for review.

   b. Essay-Type Questions

     (1) Read each question carefully.

     (2) Determine exactly what is wanted. Underline key words or phrases.

     (3) Decide on outline or paragraph answer.

     (4) Include many different points and elements unless asked to develop any one or two points or elements.

     (5) Show impartiality by giving pros and cons unless directed to select one side only.

     (6) Make and write down any assumptions you find necessary to answer the question.

     (7) Watch your English, grammar, punctuation, choice of words.

     (8) Time your answers; don't crowd material.

8. Answering the Essay Question
   Most essay questions can be answered by framing the specific response around several key words or ideas. Here are a few such key words or ideas:
   M's: manpower, materials, methods, money, management

   P's: purpose, program, policy, plan, procedure, practice, problems, pitfalls, personnel, public relations

   a. Six basic steps in handling problems:
      (1) preliminary plan and background development
      (2) collect information, data and facts
      (3) analyze and interpret information, data and facts
      (4) analyze and develop solutions as well as make recommendations
      (5) prepare report and sell recommendations
      (6) install recommendations and follow up effectiveness

   b. Pitfalls to Avoid
      (1 *Taking things for granted*
          A statement of the situation does not necessarily imply that each of the elements is necessarily true; for example, a complaint may be invalid and biased so that all that can be taken for granted is that a complaint has been registered.
      (2) *Considering only one side of a situation*
          Wherever possible, indicate several alternatives and then point out the reasons you selected the best one.
      (3) *Failing to indicate follow up*
          Whenever your answer indicates action on your part, make certain that you will take proper follow-up action to see how successful your recommendations, procedures, or actions turn out to be.
      (4) *Taking too long in answering any single question*
          Remember to time your answers properly.

EXAMINATION SECTION

EXAMINATION SECTION
TEST 1

DIRECTIONS: Each question or incomplete statement is followed by several suggested answers or completions. Select the one that *BEST* answers the question or completes the statement. *PRINT THE LETTER OF THE CORRECT ANSWER IN THE SPACE AT THE RIGHT.*

1. Exhaust noises from diesel engines are *reduced* by using   1.___
   A. accumulators   B. exhaust manifolds
   C. mufflers   D. surge suppressors

2. In a two-stroke cycle diesel engine, the cylinder is   2.___
   scavenged by the
   A. exhaust gases   B. combustion air
   C. injected fuel oil
   D. mixture of fuel oil and air

3. The *BASIC* difference between a diesel engine and a   3.___
   gasoline engine is in the
   A. fuel and ignition systems   B. cooling systems
   C. limits on horsepower output D. weight per horsepower

4. Of the following preliminary steps to be taken before   4.___
   starting a propulsion diesel engine, the one which should
   be taken *FIRST* is to
   A. line up the starting air system and roll the engine
      a few R.P.M.'s
   B. close all cylinder air cocks
   C. line up and start the pre-lube pump
   D. check all lube oil levels

5. In the four-stroke cycle diesel engine, the correct   5.___
   sequence of strokes that takes place in a cycle in the
   cylinder is:
   A. Suction, compression, expansion or power, and exhaust
      strokes
   B. Suction, expansion or power, exhaust, and compression
      strokes
   C. Exhaust, expansion or power, suction, and compression
      strokes
   D. Compression, exhaust, expansion or power, and suction
      strokes

6. As a cylinder in a diesel engine is going through its   6.___
   compression cycle, the air in the cylinder should
   A. *decrease* in pressure and *increase* in temperature
   B. *increase* in pressure and *decrease* in temperature
   C. *decrease* in pressure and *decrease* in temperature
   D. *increase* in pressure and *increase* in temperature

7. Of the following, the *one* function *NOT* provided for by   7.___
   a diesel's fuel injection system is
   A. raising the pressure of the fuel to overcome the
      cylinder pressures

B. maintaining the fuel in concentrated liquid form for maximum power

C. metering the fuel so as to assure equal quantities for all cylinders

D. introducing the fuel into the cylinders at the proper times

8. In a four-stroke diesel engine, every piston should fire every
   8.___
   A. half revolution of the crankshaft
   B. revolution of the crankshaft
   C. two revolutions of the crankshaft
   D. four revolutions of the crankshaft

9. With respect to diesel engines, the term "supercharging" refers to increasing the
   9.___
   A. fuel storage tank capacity so that more fuel may be carried
   B. total amount of fuel pumped into the working engine
   C. total amount of charging air and lubricating oil pumped into the working engine
   D. total amount of charging air pumped into the working cylinder of the engine

10. The governor on a diesel engine controls engine speed by
    10.___
    A. increasing or decreasing the fuel supply
    B. throttling the air supply to each cylinder
    C. automatically advancing the spark
    D. applying dynamic braking to, or removing it from, the shaft

11. A diesel engine is a(n)
    11.___
    A. spark ignition engine   B. expansion ignition engine
    C. compression ignition engine
    D. suction ignition engine

12. The MAIN function of an intercooler and aftercooler of an air compressor is to
    12.___
    A. condense the moisture in the compressed air
    B. remove metallic impurities from the compressor
    C. cool the water in the cylinder jacket
    D. cool the air compressor lube oil

13. A gear-type lube oil transfer pump is one that usually contains
    13.___
    A. rollers and pinions   B. D-type slide valves
    C. hydraulic plungers   D. twin gear elements

14. A pump that has no moving parts is the
    14.___
    A. rotary pump   B. centrifugal pump
    C. propeller pump   D. jet pump

15. An example of a positive-displacement pump is the
    15.___
    A. centrifugal pump   B. impeller pump
    C. gear pump   D. turbine pump

16. A precaution that should be taken prior to the start-up   16.___
    of a positive displacement pump so as to prevent damaging
    the pump or its output lines is to make sure that the
    A. suction valve is open   B. discharge valve is open
    C. bypass valve is closed
    D. pump has been properly primed

17. The *MAIN* reason a duplex strainer is installed in most   17.___
    lubricating and fuel oil pipe lines is to
    A. double the amount of oil flow through the strainer
    B. permit one strainer to be removed and cleaned without
       disturbing the oil flow
    C. reduce maintenance costs by allowing both strainers
       to be removed and cleaned at the same time
    D. make sure that the oil flow is being strained twice

18. Spur, bevel, helical, and worm are words used to describe 18.___
    various types of
    A. steel cables   B. shut-off valves
    C. shaft seals   D. gear shapes

19. A metal *commonly* used for bearing linings is   19.___
    A. babbitt   B. Muntz metal
    C. duraluminum   D. naval brass

20. Zinc plugs or plates are introduced into a salt water   20.___
    cooling system in order to
    A. prevent the formation of salt deposits
    B. counteract the electrolytic action between dissimilar
       metals
    C. close holes or patch cracks that may have developed
    D. attract and hold metallic particles in the water

KEY (CORRECT ANSWERS)

1.	C	11.	C
2.	B	12.	A
3.	A	13.	D
4.	D	14.	D
5.	A	15.	C
6.	D	16.	B
7.	B	17.	B
8.	C	18.	D
9.	D	19.	A
10.	A	20.	B

TEST 2

DIRECTIONS: Each question or incomplete statement is followed by several suggested answers or completions. Select the one that *BEST* answers the question or completes the statement. *PRINT THE LETTER OF THE CORRECT ANSWER IN THE SPACE AT THE RIGHT.*

1. Of the following pipe fittings, the *one* that should be used to connect a 2½" diameter pipe to a 3" diameter pipe is a(n)
    A. offset   B. sleeve   C. union   D. increaser   1.___

2. A 4"-long piece of 3/4"-diameter brass pipe threaded on the outside at *both* ends is called a
    A. stud   B. nipple   C. coupling   D. lintel   2.___

3. Of the following valves, the *one* which should be used for throttling purposes is the
    A. check valve   B. globe valve
    C. gate valve   D. relief valve   3.___

4. An "automatic temperature regulator" installed in a cooling system is known as a
    A. one-way proportioning valve
    B. two-way proportioning valve
    C. three-way proportioning valve
    D. four-way proportioning valve   4.___

5. A gate valve is rated as "WOG 300." The letters WOG mean
    A. Water, Oil, or Gas   B. Wrought iron or Galvanized
    C. Worthington or Galveston   D. With oil tight gaskets   5.___

6. A machine screw is designated as an "8-32." The number 32 represents the
    A. number of threads per inch
    B. outside diameter in centimeters
    C. length in inches
    D. finish and metal of construction   6.___

7. When a flanged joint in a high temperature piping system must be broken often, the gaskets are coated with a substance to prevent them from sticking to the face flange. Of the following substances, the *one* which is *most commonly* used for coating gaskets for this purpose is
    A. #6 fuel oil   B. water resistant grease
    C. powdered graphite   D. caustic soda   7.___

8. Ethylene glycol is added to fresh water in a closed cooling piping system *MAINLY* to
    A. combat sludge formations in the system
    B. change the freezing and boiling points of the water
    C. neutralize acidity of the water
    D. provide lubrication for moving parts in the system   8.___

9. "Unloaders" are *generally* found on
    A. flexible couplings   B. surge suppressors
    C. centrifugal pumps   D. air compressors   9.___

10. A Bourdon gauge is used to measure 10.___
    A. pressure   B. contaminants
    C. temperature   D. distance

11. Emergency generators aboard ship are located 11.___
    A. *adjacent to* the steering gear room
    B. *next to* the main electrical control panel
    C. *topside* above deck
    D. *in* the machinery spaces

12. In a diesel engine that has ten cylinders, the number of 12.___
cylinders that are *usually* equipped with an air-starting
valve is
    A. 2   B. 3   C. 5   D. 10

13. A device used to connect or disconnect at will a part 13.___
which transmits power to or from a rotating shaft is
called a
    A. coupling   B. union   C. clutch   D. splice

14. Of the following solvents, the *one* that should be used 14.___
to clean a paint brush that has been used with oil paint
is
    A. mineral spirits   B. alcohol
    C. carbon tetrachloride   D. trichlorethylene

15. "Red lead" is a preparation that is applied to 15.___
    A. boat hulls below the water line to prevent "fouling"
    B. outdoor woodwork to make it more resistant to the
       weather
    C. tin, iron and steelwork as a rust preventive
    D. metal surfaces to give them a high gloss finish

16. Silver solder is *often* used to make up solder joints in 16.___
    A. black steel pipe   B. copper tubing
    C. cast iron pipe   D. aluminum tubing

17. A chemical solution used to test for the presence of 17.___
salt water in lubricating oil is
    A. brine   B. hydrochloric acid
    C. silver nitrate   D. acetic acid

18. To properly clean the sea water passages of a shell-and- 18.___
tube type lube oil cooler, an oiler should use
    A. an air or water lance   B. a straight wire brush
    C. rubber plugs having attached metal scrapers
    D. a tapered steel bar

19. The *MAIN* function of the element used in a lube oil 19.___
filter is to trap
    A. oil additives   B. dirt and sludge
    C. oil vapors   D. fuel oil

20. A lubricating oil designated as S.A.E. 10 is *generally* 20.___
considered to be a(n) _____ oil.
    A. light   B. medium-heavy
    C. heavy   D. extra-heavy

KEY (CORRECT ANSWERS)

1.	D	11.	C
2.	B	12.	D
3.	B	13.	C
4.	C	14.	A
5.	A	15.	C
6.	A	16.	B
7.	C	17.	C
8.	B	18.	A
9.	D	19.	B
10.	A	20.	A

EXAMINATION SECTION

TEST 1

DIRECTIONS   Each question or incomplete statement is followed by
several suggested answers or completions. Select the
one that *BEST* answers the question or completes the
statement. *PRINT THE LETTER OF THE CORRECT ANSWER IN
THE SPACE AT THE RIGHT.*

1. Of the following diesel injection systems, the one which   1.___
   is *SELDOM* used, and then only for large engines using
   heavy viscous fuels, is the
      A. common-rail system   B. individual-pump system
      C. distributor system   D. air-injection system

2. An engine indicator is an instrument that is used to   2.___
   determine the
      A. operating speed of the engine
      B. temperature in an engine
      C. oil pressure in an engine
      D. performance of the engine

3. The *MOST* accurate method of determining whether there are   3.___
   cracks in the crankshafts of diesel engines is to use
      A. chalk and alcohol   B. magnaflux
      C. electrolysis   D. copper sulfate solution

4. The *MAIN* function of a mechanical clutch on a direct-   4.___
   drive propulsion diesel engine is to provide a means for
      A. disconnecting the engine from the propeller shaft
      B. reversing the direction of rotation of the propeller
         shaft
      C. reducing the operating speed
      D. obtaining a low propeller-shaft speed with a high
         engine speed

5. Of the following, the one which is *NOT* used to start a   5.___
   diesel engine in an emergency is compressed
      A. air   B. nitrogen   C. carbon dioxide   D. oxygen

6. In comparing the exhaust temperatures of a two stroke-   6.___
   cycle diesel engine with that of a four-stroke-cycle
   diesel engine, the exhaust temperature of a two-stroke-
   cycle diesel engine is
      A. the same as that of the four-stroke-cycle engine
      B. lower than that of the four-stroke-cycle engine
      C. higher than that of the four-stroke-cycle engine
      D. either higher or lower than that of the four-stroke-
         cycle engine depending on the relative size of the
         engines

7. If the fluid level in a closed system cooling system expan- 7.___
   sion tank is low, it should be replenished with
      A. pure ethylene glycol   B. sea water
      C. distilled water   D. Zeolite

8. The differential needle valve injection nozzles of a   8.___
diesel engine are opened by
   A. a spring force   B. the cam mechanism
   C. the fuel oil pressure D. a solenoid mechanism

9. The *MAIN* reason for using filters in the fuel oil system   9.___
of a diesel engine is to
   A. remove vanadium and sodium from the oil
   B. protect the injectors and the injection pumps
   C. protect the booster pumps
   D. remove water from the fuel oil

10. An oiler cleaning plugged diesel fuel injector orifices   10.___
should use
   A. acetone   B. music wire
   C. steam pressure   D. hot water

11. In a common rail fuel injection system, timing is con-   11.___
trolled by the
   A. injector cam only   B. fuel pump only
   C. wedge only   D. injector cam and the wedge

12. The *MAIN* bearings of a reciprocating engine are classified 12.___
as
   A. thrust bearings   B. angular bearings
   C. radial bearings   D. guide bearings

13. Proper vacuum will be maintained in the main condenser   13.___
of a reciprocating steam engine propulsion plant when the
condenser overboard discharge temperature is kept below
the temperature corresponding to the vacuum by *APPROXIMATELY*
   A. 1 to 3 degrees F.   B. 5 to 8 degrees F.
   C. 10 to 12 degrees F.   D. 12 to 14 degrees F.

14. When propulsion reciprocating steam engines are fitted   14.___
with forced lubrication and are not in operation or under
repair, oil should be circulated through the lube oil
system for at least 15 minutes
   A. daily   B. every 2 days
   C. every 4 days   D. weekly

15. On a multi-expansion counterflow reciprocating steam   15.___
engine, by-passes to the receivers are used when
   A. warming-up the engine
   B. frequent stopping and reversing of the engine is
      expected
   C. taking a cylinder out of service
   D. securing the engine

16. A pyrometer is used for measuring   16.___
   A. pressure B. vacuum   C. temperature D. viscosity

17. Clearance pocket valves on uniflow reciprocating steam   17.___
engines are opened when
   A. the engine is running at maximum speed
   B. warming-up the engine
   C. boiler carryover has occurred
   D. there is a loss of vacuum

18. Of the following, the one that would cause a loss of   18.___
vacuum in the main condenser of a multi-expansion counterflow reciprocating steam engine installation is
    A. operating the main condenser circulating pump too fast
    B. excessively worn high pressure cylinder piston
       rod packing
    C. excessive use of cylinder lubrication
    D. operating the main condenser condensate pump too fast

19. The *MAIN* purpose of the oil groves in a reciprocating   19.___
steam engine bearing is to
    A. promote distribution of lube oil in the bearing
    B. prevent pressure build-up in the bearing
    C. ensure proper flow of oil out of the bearing
    D. allow space for locating a thermometer well

20. Steam admission valves used in a propulsion uniflow   20.___
reciprocating steam engine are of the
    A. Corliss valve type   B. slide valve type
    C. poppet valve type   D. piston valve type

21. Cylinders of propulsion uniflow steam engines are   21.___
lubricated from
    A. a gravity feed system
    B. the same system that lubricates the engine bearings
    C. a splash feed system
    D. mechanical lubricators

22. Steam admission valves installed on propulsion steam   22.___
engines of the uniflow type are operated by
    A. one cam shaft   B. two parallel cam shafts
    C. individual eccentric sheaves and rods
    D. individual eccentric sheaves and wristplates

23. Intercoolers and aftercoolers are fitted to most air   23.___
compressor installations in order to
    A. cool the cylinder jacket water
    B. cool the air compressor lube oil
    C. condense the moisture from compressed air
    D. remove metal impurities from the compressor

24. The difference between an open and a closed feedwater   24.___
heater is that
    A. the closed heater is vented and the open heater is
       uncovered
    B. the open heater is used with high temperatures and
       the closed heater is used with low temperatures
    C. steam and water are at different pressures in the
       open heater and are at the same pressure in closed
       heaters
    D. steam and water are directly mixed in the open
       heater and are not mixed in the closed heater

25. Of the following types of pumps, the one which does *NOT*   25.___
have moving parts is the
    A. jet pump   B. propeller pump
    C. centrifugal pump   D. rotary pump

26. Of the following, the one which is *NOT* a common use for   26.___
    compressed air aboard ship is
    A. starting diesel engines
    B. operating automatic combustion control systems
    C. operating pneumatic tools
    D. supplying secondary air to the firebox

27. Marine centrifugal pumps have impellers which *USUALLY*   27.___
    rotate
    A. in the direction of the vane curvature (forward curved)
    B. in the direction opposite to the vane curvature
       (backward curved)
    C. in either direction
    D. at twice motor speed

28. Of the following methods, the one which is *NOT* used to   28.___
    allow for the expansion of condenser tubes is the use of
    A. ferrules   B. bowed tubes
    C. shell expansion joints   D. tube knuckles

29. Of the following fittings, the one which is *NOT* found on   29.___
    the steam side of a condenser is a
    A. drain well gage glass   B. sentinel valve
    C. zinc plate anode   D. vacuum gage

30. The operation of a condensate pump when the level of the   30.___
    water in the drain well is low will *MOST* probably result in
    A. too high a level in the D.C. heater
    B. excessive discharge pressure
    C. pump cavitation   D. loss of condensate level

31. Pounding in the liquid end of a reciprocating steam pump   31.___
    would *NOT* be caused by
    A. tight packing in the liquid end
    B. improper adjustment of the steam cushioning valves
    C. a loose liquid piston
    D. loose water chest valves

32. The *CORRECT* procedure to lower the salinity of boiler   32.___
    water is to
    A. add boiler compound
    B. add chloride ions
    C. pass the boiler water through an ultraviolet purifier
    D. "blow down" the boiler

33. In an automatic packaged boiler, a condition which will   33.___
    NOT cause the fuel oil solenoid valve to close is
    A. low water level   B. high oil pressure
    C. high steam pressure   D. low voltage

34. Of the following, the one which is *NOT* a heat recovery   34.___
    unit is a(n)
    A. spark arrester   B. exhaust boiler
    C. stack mounted hot water heater
    D. exhaust gas heated evaporator

35. Of the following materials, the one which is *NOT* used for water lubricated stern tube bearings is

    A. lignum vitae   B. rubber
    C. babbitt
    D. laminated resin bonded composition

35.___

36. The pump used with an electro-hydraulic steering gear is a

    A. screw pump   B. variable stroke pump
    C. gear pump   D. lobe pump

36.___

37. The device that is used to change over hydraulic pumps on electro-hydraulic steering gears is a

    A. differential valve   B. shuttle valve
    C. six-way valve   D. check valve

37.___

38. The telemotor receiver signal of an electro-hydraulic steering gear is used

    A. to directly set the variable stroke pump
    B. to start or stop the pump motors
    C. to turn the six-way valve
    D. as an input signal to the differential follow-up control

38.___

39. Hot packing glands on a centrifugal pump are *NOT* caused by

    A. tight packing   B. plugged lantern rings
    C. excessive water leakage D. a scored shaft

39.___

40. A "hunting" governor on an engine

    A. maintains a steady engine rpm
    B. maintains a lower rpm of the engine than required
    C. permits the engine to alternately race and slow down
    D. maintains a higher rpm of the engine than required

40.___

KEY (CORRECT ANSWERS)

#		#		#		#	
1.	D	11.	D	21.	D	31.	A
2.	D	12.	A	22.	B	32.	D
3.	B	13.	B	23.	C	33.	B
4.	A	14.	A	24.	D	34.	A
5.	D	15.	A	25.	A	35.	C
6.	B	16.	C	26.	D	36.	B
7.	C	17.	D	27.	B	37.	B
8.	C	18.	C	28.	D	38.	D
9.	B	19.	A	29.	C	39.	C
10.	B	20.	C	30.	C	40.	C

TEST 2

DIRECTIONS: Each question or incomplete statement is followed by several suggested answers or completions. Select the one that *BEST* answers the question or completes the statement. *PRINT THE LETTER OF THE CORRECT ANSWER IN THE SPACE AT THE RIGHT.*

1. A centrifugal pump should be started with the   1.____
   - A. suction and the discharge valves open
   - B. suction and the discharge valves closed
   - C. suction valve closed and the discharge valve open
   - D. suction valve open and the discharge valve closed

2. In a high pressure turbine installation, condenser vacuum   2.____
   is maintained by an
   - A. air and condensate pump   B. air injector
   - C. air ejector   D. air eductor

3. The *MAIN* reason why most reciprocating pumps are fitted   3.____
   with air chambers is to
   - A. provide a steady discharge pressure
   - B. prime the suction side of the pump
   - C. seal the liquid end piston rod packing glands
   - D. cushion the liquid piston

4. Propeller thrust is *GENERALLY* absorbed by a(n)   4.____
   - A. Westinghouse type bearing   B. antifriction bearing
   - C. Kingsbury type bearing   D. Hele-Shaw type bearing

5. Gland sealing steam is provided on turbines exhausting to   5.____
   a condenser in order to prevent
   - A. loss of vacuum   B. reduction of shaft speed
   - C. overheating of seal   D. breakdown of carbon packing

6. The *MAXIMUM* temperature at which a turbine bearing may   6.____
   satisfactorily operate is
   - A. 120°F.   B. 180°F.   C. 220°F.   D. 250°F.

7. The type of turbine governor which closes the throttle   7.____
   valve and stops the turbine when the turbine speed reaches
   10% in excess of normal speed is called a(n)
   - A. emergency governor   B. constant speed governor
   - C. speed limiting governor   D. load limiting governor

8. A turbo-generator lube oil cooler should be put into   8.____
   operation
   - A. as soon as the turbine is started
   - B. before the turbine is started
   - C. when the sump oil temperature is at 140°F.
   - D. when the temperature of the hottest bearing reaches 100°F.

9. The suction and discharge valves of an air compressor   9.____
   should be cleaned with
   - A. soap suds   B. kerosene
   - C. gasoline   D. carbon tetrachloride

10. Lubrication for modern air compressors is supplied by   10.___
     A. a gravity feed   B. grease cups
     C. a wick feed
     D. an oil pump attached to air compressor shaft

11. Sealed stern tube bearings are lubricated with   11.___
     A. water   B. lube oil   C. tallow   D. fish oil

12. Of the following hand operated valves, the one which is   12.___
    BEST suited for regulating or controlling fluid flow is the
     A. non-rising stem gate valve   B. rising stem gate valve
     C. globe valve   D. quick closing valve

13. It would be physically impossible to open the throttle   13.___
    valve when starting a turbo-generator set before the
     A. condensate pump is started
     B. circulating pump is started
     C. turbine casing and throttle drains are open
     D. hand lube oil pump is operated

14. Of the following types of Bourdon tube gages, the one   14.___
    which is commonly used for indicating the pressure drop
    between the inlet side and the outlet side of a lube oil
    strainer is the
     A. simplex type   B. vacuum type
     C. duplex type   D. compound type

15. The function of a turbine feed pump governor is to   15.___
    hold the
     A. pump discharge pressure constant as the flow varies
     B. turbine speed constant as the load varies
     C. flow through the pump constant as the discharge
       pressure varies
     D. load constant as the turbine speed varies

16. Of the following the *BEST* action to take if there is   16.___
    brush sparking on the commutator of an operating motor is to
     A. stop the motor   B. change the motor speed
     C. reverse the direction of rotation
     D. report this condition to the marine engineer of the
       watch

17. The bearings installed in electric motors from 1 to 200   17.___
    horsepower are, *GENERALLY*,
     A. bronze bushing type bearings
     B. ball or roller type bearings
     C. babbitt type bearings   D. sleeve type bearings

18. Turbine reduction gear surfaces receive lubricating oil   18.___
     A. from spray nozzles   B. by splash lubrication
     C. by gears dipping in sump oil   D. from oil rings

19. While under way, strainers used in forced feed lubrication 19.___
    systems should be cleaned *EVERY*
     A. 4 hours   B. 12 hours   C. 18 hours   D. 24 hours

20. A device used for deadening or silencing exhaust noises   20.___
    from a diesel engine is called a(n)
        A. air blower   B. exhaust manifold
        C. tail pipe   D. muffler

21. The API Service Classification "Service DM" pertains to   21.___
    a grease used for
        A. gasoline engines   B. diesel engines
        C. direct current generators or motors
        D. reciprocating pumps

22. Of the following types of lubricating materials the   22.___
    BEST type to use for modern machinery operating at high
    speeds and high temperatures is
        A. animal   B. vegetable   C. water   D. mineral

23. Lubricating oil viscosities   23.___
        A. decrease with a temperature decrease
        B. decrease with a temperature increase
        C. increase with a temperature increase
        D. remain constant regardless of temperature changes

24. In order to clean a metal edge type filter, an oiler   24.___
    would
        A. operate the cleaner blades B. wash the filter in kerosene
        C. throw out the element   D. change the basket

25. Detergents are used in lubricating oils to   25.___
        A. prevent rusting of ferrous surface
        B. prevent formation of sludge deposits
        C. prevent oxidation of oil D. control oil foaming

26. The designation SAE 30 of a lubricating oil refers to its 26.___
        A. ability to vaporize   B. value as an anti-oxidant
        C. viscosity   D. anti-corrosion additives

27. Of the following the one which is *NOT* normally a cause of 27.___
    lube oil contamination in a diesel engine is
        A. fuel oil burning on the cylinder walls
        B. dust entering the air intake system
        C. leaky crankcase seals
        D. dilution by the fuel oil

28. Lube oil pressure regulator valves usually "dump" oil   28.___
    from the lube oil
        A. cooler inlet to lube oil cooler outlet
        B. pump discharge to filter
        C. header to sump
        D. cooler inlet to sump

29. Of the following, the one which is *NOT* a function of   29.___
    lubricating oils in diesel engines is to
        A. assist in sealing the piston-cylinder wall clearance
        B. act as a vibration absorber
        C. clean and carry away dirt or metal particles from
           bearing
        D. act as a cooling agent

30. Of the following fluids, the one that should be used to   30.___
    clean filtering bags of pressure type lube oil filters is
    A. gasoline   B. carbon tetrachloride
    C. kerosene   D. bunker "C"

31. The fluid used as a sealing agent in lube oil centrifuges   31.___
    is
    A. kerosene   B. ethylene glycol
    C. magnesium sulfate brine   D. water

32. A good surface film on the commutators and the slip   32.___
    rings of electrical generators is indicated when the
    surface film color appears
    A. gray   B. brown
    C. jet black   D. bright copper

33. Assume that you are an oiler on an engine room watch and   33.___
    you hear a continuous ringing of the general alarm bell
    for more than 10 seconds. Your FIRST action should be to
    A. see that water is supplied to the deck fire line
    B. leave the engine room
    C. go to the boat station
    D. assist in securing the propulsion unit

34. In disposing of a small amount of waste oil you should   34.___
    A. carefully pour it into the engine room bilge well
    B. put it into a 5 gallon container, seal, and drop it
       over the ship's side
    C. pour it into the waste rag can
    D. pour it into an oil slop tank

35. Assume that a fireman pulled a "live" burner. The FIRST   35.___
    thing you as an   oiler should do in this case is to
    A. leave the fireroom   B. sound the alarm
    C. shut off the oil supply   D. call the engineer.

36. Assume that the CO_2 alarm sounded in a space where you are 36.___
    working. You should
    A. immediately leave the area
    B. finish what you are doing and then leave the area
    C. signal to the bridge that you heard the alarm
    D. wait for a second alarm bell to ring before taking
       any action

37. Of the following when extinguishing a burning liquid with 37.___
    a portable foam type extinguisher, the stream of foam
    should NOT be directed
    A. against the back wall of the vat or tank just above
       the burning surface
    B. into the burning liquid
    C. on the floor just in front of the burning area
    D. from far enough away to allow it to fall lightly
       upon the burning surface

Questions 38 - 40.

DIRECTIONS: Questions numbered from 38 to 40 inclusive refer to the sketch shown below of a main condenser circulating water system.

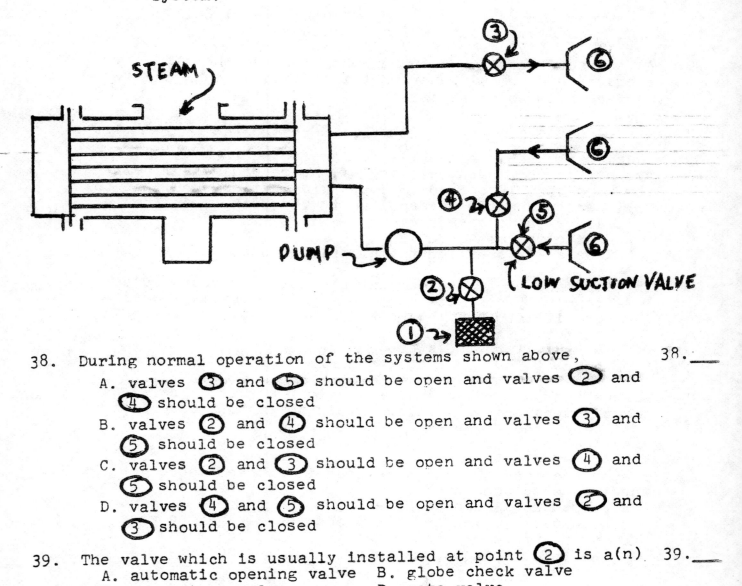

38.   During normal operation of the systems shown above,   38.____
   A. valves ③ and ⑤ should be open and valves ② and ④ should be closed
   B. valves ② and ④ should be open and valves ③ and ⑤ should be closed
   C. valves ② and ③ should be open and valves ④ and ⑤ should be closed
   D. valves ④ and ⑤ should be open and valves ② and ③ should be closed

39.   The valve which is usually installed at point ② is a(n) 39.____
      A. automatic opening valve   B. globe check valve
      C. non-return valve   D. gate valve

40.   The parts numbered ⑥ are   40.____
      A. sea chests
      C. manifolds   B. tanks
                                   D. headers

KEY (CORRECT ANSWERS)

1.	D	11.	B	21.	B	31.	D
2.	C	12.	C	22.	D	32.	B
3.	A	13.	D	23.	B	33.	A
4.	C	14.	C	24.	A	34.	D
5.	A	15.	A	25.	B	35.	C
6.	B	16.	D	26.	C	36.	A
7.	A	17.	B	27.	C	37.	B
8.	D	18.	A	28.	C	38.	A
9.	A	19.	A	29.	B	39.	C
10.	D	20.	D	30.	C	40.	A

EXAMINATION SECTION
TEST 1

DIRECTIONS: Each question or incomplete statement is followed by several suggested answers or completions. Select the one that BEST answers the question or completes the statement.

1. Of the following lubricating greases, the one that is generally known as a heat-resisting grease is
   A. soda (sodium) soap grease
   B. lime (calcium) soap grease
   C. aluminum soap grease
   D. mixed (soda and lime) grease

2. The chassis grease recommended for MOST pieces of construction equipment is generally
   A. lime base-water resistant
   B. SAE-140 E.P.
   C. number 3 cup
   D. number 2 cup

3. The PRIMARY advantage that a friction clutch has over a positive clutch is that the friction clutch
   A. runs at lower speeds
   B. requires less maintenance
   C. can be engaged at either low or high speeds
   D. runs at high speeds

4. Of the following makes of power plants for cranes, the one which uses diesel fuel is the
   A. Allis-Chalmers L-525   B. G.M. 4055-C
   C. Waukesha 140 GKU
   D. Waukesha 140 GKU (with torque converter)

5. In a 2 stroke cycle diesel engine, the cylinder is scavenged by
   A. the combustion air
   B. the exhaust gases
   C. the injected fuel oil
   D. a mixture of fuel oil and air

6. In a 6 X 19 Seale wire rope, the wires in one strand are
   A. always of the same size
   B. of different diameters
   C. meshed with soft cores
   D. of the flattened strand type

7. Of the following metals, the one that is USUALLY used for socketing wire ropes is
      A. lead   B. tin   C. zinc   D. 50-50 solder

8. On the suction stroke of a four stroke cycle full diesel engine
   A. fuel oil only is drawn into the cylinder
   B. air and a full charge of fuel oil are drawn into the cylinder
   C. air only is drawn into the cylinder
   D. air and a one-half charge of fuel oil are drawn into the cylinder

9. The PRIMARY purpose of crossing a belt when connecting two pulleys is to
   A. rotate the shafts in opposite directions
   B. decrease the belt friction contact
   C. be able to use a thinner belt
   D. increase the overall belt efficiency

10. Double-base safety clips having corrugated jaws when used on wire rope in making up an eye develops approximately
    A. 60% of the strength of the rope
    B. 70% of the strength of the rope
    C. 80% of the strength of the rope
    D. 95% of the strength of the rope

11. The number of ropes usually used on the movable block of a 4 part fall is MOST NEARLY
    A. 6   B. 4   C. 3   D. 2

Question 12.

DIRECTION: Question number 12 is based on the sketch below :

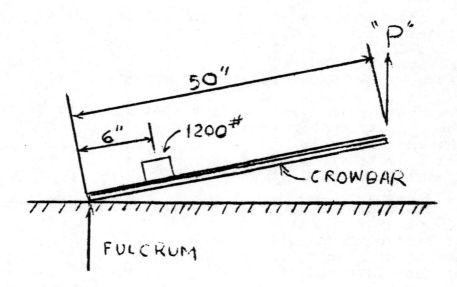

12. In the above sketch, the left "P" in pounds required to raise the 1200 pound block from the ground is MOST NEARLY
    A. 200   B. 160   C. 144   D. 96

13. In the common rail system of solid fuel injection in a Diesel engine, a control wedge is generally used to
    A. control the lift of the mechanically operated spray valve
    B. meter the fuel oil at the transfer pump
    C. control the fuel oil level in the fuel tank
    D. fix the fuel oil pressure in the "common rail"

14. In the fuel system for a 4-stroke cycle full diesel engine the oil travels in sequence from the fuel tank to the
    A. filters, transfer pump, pre-combustion chamber, injection pump, and injection valve
    B. filters, transfer pump, pre-combustion chamber, injection valve, and injection pump
    C. transfer pump, filters, injection pump, injection valve, and pre-combustion chamber
    D. filters, injection pump, transfer pump, injection valve, and pre-combustion chamber

15. The cam shaft operating the valves of a 4-stroke cycle diesel engine rotates at
    A. the same speed as the crankshaft
    B. half the speed of the crankshaft
    C. double the speed of the crankshaft
    D. four times the speed of the crankshaft

16. The speed of a crane trolley motor is 1200 r.p,m. If the motor pinion has 24 teeth and the driven gear has 92 teeth, the speed of the gear shaft is MOST NEARLY
    A. 250   B. 300   C. 350   D. 3600

17. In a 4-stroke cycle full diesel engine, the fuel is ignited by means of
    A. special spark plugs
    B. hot exhaust gases
    C. highly compressed air in the cylinder
    D. glow plugs in the cylinder heads

18. The proper gap on a spark plug can be MOST accurately set by use of a
    A. dial gage
    B. conventional flat feeler gage
    C. square wire feeler gage
    D. round wire feeler gage

19. A considerable amount of water in the crankcase of a gasoline engine would NOT be likely due to
    A. a cylinder head crack   B. cylinder head gasket leaks
    C. cylinder block cracks   D. condensation

20. A good program of preventive maintenance would NOT require
    A. having the work done in an "off" shift
    B. periodic inspection
    C. cleaning the equipment before servicing
    D. accurate records of the servicing done

21. The MAXIMUM ampere rating of the fuse to be used in an existing circuit depends upon the
    A. size of wire in the circuit
    B. connected load
    C. voltage of the line
    D. rating of the switch

22. On a truck mounted portable air compressor, the differential assembly is located in the
    A. truck transmission housing
    B. air compressor crankcase
    C. truck rear housing
    D. air regulating equipment

23. In operation, a gasoline driven air compressor is said to be unloaded when
    A. the air compressor is driven at low speed
    B. the discharge valves on the air compressor are held in the open position
    C. the safety valve on the air compressor is engaged in the open position
    D. the inlet valves on the air compressor are held in the open position

24. In reference to air controlled machines operating in mid-winter, the reservoir of the anti-freezer or evaporator should be filled with
    A. methyl alcohol   B. ethyl alcohol
    C. an alcohol containing an inhibitor   D. prestone

25. A grade of 1 in 20 is approximately the same as a
    A. 1 foot rise in a 200 inch run
    B. 1 yard rise in a 125 yard run
    C. 10 inch rise in a 200 yard run
    D. 12 inch rise in a 7 yard run

26. The minimum factor of safety of a wire rope that is used for grab buckets should be NOT less than
    A. 4   B. 6   C. 8   D. 10

27. Whenever possible, it is BEST to remove a gear from a shaft by means of
    A. heating the gear with a flame
    B. heavy but uniform blows with a hammer
    C. cooling the shaft with dry ice
    D. an appropriate wheel puller

28. For digging open cuts, drainage ditches, and gravel pits, where the material is to be moved from 20 to 3000 feet before dumping, one would use a
    A. Crawler Crane Excavator   B. Gantry Crane Excavator
    C. Drag-line Excavator   D. Diesel Shovel Excavator

29. If a bucket capable of carrying 5 3/4 cubic yards is loaded to
    3/4 of its capacity, it will be carrying, in cubic yards,
    APPROXIMATELY
    A. 3 1/2   B. 4 1/4   C. 4 7/8   D. 5 1/4

30. A guy line is generally used with a
    A. diesel driven scraper   B. stiff leg derrick
    C. truck mounted clamshell   D. gantry crane

31. The point shaft on a boom is usually located near the
    A. top of the boom   B. bottom of the boom
    C. dead end cable socket   D. hoist drum

32. Assume that a horizontal roller chain drive is used to transmit
    power to the jack shaft of a crane. For proper tension in the
    roller chain
    A. there should be a small amount of sag in the chain
    B. the sag should bring the chain down to the center line of
       the driving sprocket
    C. there should be no sag in the chain
    D. the chain should make an angle of at least 50° when leaving
       the driving sprocket

Question 33.

DIRECTIONS: Question number 33 is based on the sketch below:

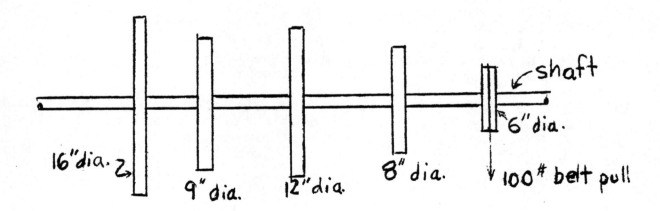

33. In reference to the above sketch, in order to balance the 100 lbs
    belt pull on the 6" diameter pulley, a belt pull of approximate-
    ly 67 lbs. should be attached to which one of the following pul-
    leys?
    A. 16"   B. 12"   C. 9"   D. 8"

34. Of the following statements concerning torque converter equipped machines, the one which is MOST NEARLY CORRECT is that
    A. the torque converter is a transmission with a limited number of ratios
    B. at normal speeds, the line pulls are less than on a standard mechanical drive machine
    C. the shock loading is increased during shovel operations
    D. at stall conditions, the engine is "putting out" its maximum power

35. To transmit power between two shafts that are in the same plane but 90° to each other, it is BEST to use
    A. spur gears
    B. worm and spur gear
    C. bevel gears
    D. herringbone gears

36. Under normal operations, the oil pressure regulating valve piston on a torque converter should be removed and cleaned once
    A. a day   B. a week   C. a month   D. every three months

37. The operating oil pressure in a torque converter usually has a range of approximately
    A. 15 to 20 psi
    B. 35 to 40 psi
    C. 50 to 65 psi
    D. 70 to 85 psi

38. For successful operation of a machine equipped with a torque converter, the operator should
    A. watch the load or bucket
    B. listen to the engine
    C. vary the output shaft governor setting
    D. vary the engine governor setting

39. The clutch torque delivered by a fluid coupling is APPROXIMATELY
    A. the same as the engine torque
    B. twice that of the engine torque
    C. three times that of the engine torque
    D. four times that of the engine torque

40. The type of knot that can be used for shortening a rope which does not have free ends, without cutting the rope, is called a
    A. Sheet bend
    B. Hawser bend
    C. Sheepshank
    D. Clove hitch

KEY (CORRECT ANSWERS)

1.	A		21.	A
2.	A		22.	C
3.	C		23.	D
4.	B		24.	A
5.	A		25.	D
6.	B		26.	B
7.	C		27.	D
8.	C		28.	C
9.	A		29.	B
10.	D		30.	B
11.	B		31.	A
12.	C		32.	A
13.	A		33.	C
14.	C		34.	D
15.	B		35.	C
16.	B		36.	B
17.	C		37.	B
18.	D		38.	A
19.	D		39.	A
20.	A		40.	C

———

TEST 2

DIRECTIONS: Each question or incomplete statement is followed by several suggested answers or completions. Select the one that BEST answers the question or completes the statement.

1. The purpose of the hand operated choke on a gasoline engine is to
   A. provide an excess amount of air for easy starting
   B. provide a rich mixture for starting
   C. increase the jet opening for more gasoline
   D. provide a lean mixture for starting

2. In reference to gasoline engines, a common cause of engine back pressure is a
   A. corroded muffler   B. corroded exhaust pipe
   C. loose muffler   D. clogged muffler passage

3. A "Right" Lang Lay wire rope has
   A. wires and strands laid opposite to one another
   B. the wires laid left and the strands laid right
   C. both wires and strands laid to the right
   D. the wires laid right and the strands laid left

4. An ambidextrous operator during his working hours will MOST likely
   A. handle his controls with ease
   B. handle his controls slowly
   C. be handicapped in lifting loads
   D. understand instructions easily

5. Assume that a two leg bridle sling with hooks and 5/8 inch diameter ropes has a safe load capacity of 4.4 tons when the legs are in a vertical position. If the legs are set at 90% to each other, the safe load capacity in tons, of this sling is MOST NEARLY
   A. 6.2   B. 4.4   C. 3.1   D. 2.2

6. Fires in and around electrical equipment are BEST extinguished by using
   A. water   B. sand   C. carbon dioxide
   D. soda acid chemical solution

7. A dipper trip assembly is USUALLY found on a
   A. shovel boom   B. crane boom
   C. drag-line boom   D. clamshell boom

8. A convenient practical method of checking if the spark plugs in a gasoline engine are firing is to
   A. use a high tension volt meter
   B. short them with an insulated handle screw driver
   C. replace the spark plugs one at a time in the order of firing
   D. use a high tension ammeter across each spark plug

9. In a two-stage air compressor, if numbers are given to components as follows: 1st stage cylinder (1), 2nd stage cylinder(2),
   receiver tank (3), and intercooler (4); the path of the air
   when compressor is operating would be
   A. 1,2,4,3   B. 4,1,2,3
   C. 1,3,2,4   D. 1,4,2,3

10. When a lead acid type battery is fully charged, the hydrometer
    reading should be APPROXIMATELY
    A. 1.280   B. 1.190   C. 1.150   D. 1.000

11. If battery acid comes into contact with the skin the BEST thing
    to do is
    A. wipe the contact area with a piece of cloth
    B. wash away with large quantities of water
    C. wash away with a salt solution
    C. place a tourniquet above the contact area

Question 12.

DIRECTIONS: Question number 12 is based on the sketch below:

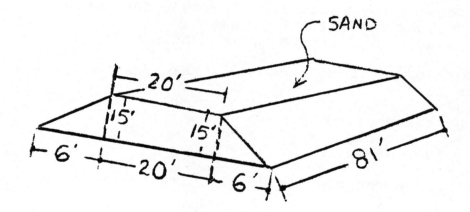

12. Assume that a section of a sand barge is uniformally loaded
    with sand as shown above. The total number of cubic yards of
    sand in this section is MOST NEARLY
    A. 120   B. 790   C. 1170   D. 2260

13. With reference to a gasoline-driven air compressor, the term
    "CFM" refers to the
    A. gasoline consumption of the engine
    B. type of unloader used on the compressor
    C. capacity of the compressor
    D. maximum revolutions of the compressor

14. Backfiring through the carburetor of a gasoline engine may MOST likely be caused by
    A. an advanced spark
    B. a blown cylinder head gasket
    C. poor combustion
    D. a defective condenser

15. Vapor-lock in a gasoline engine is MOST likely due to
    A. fuel forming bubbles in the gas line
    B. the carburetor being clogged with dirt
    C. an over rich gas-air mixture
    D. a break in the fuel pump diaphragm.

16. Of the following lubricating greases, the one that is water-resistant and can be used where the operating temperature does not exceed 175°F. is
    A. lime (calcium) soap grease
    B. soda (sodium) soap grease
    C. aluminum soap grease
    D. mixed (soda and lime) grease

17. The speed regulation of an A.C. wound rotor induction motor is B
BEST obtained by
    A. using a diverter
    B. varying the resistance in the rotor circuit
    C. varying the stator voltage
    D. rotating the brushes on the slip rings

18. The type of A.C. motor commonly used for powering electric cranes is the
    A. slip-ring type induction motor
    B. synchronous motor
    C. squirrel-cage type induction motor
    D. universal motor

19. A dash pot arrangement on a circuit breaker or motor starter USUALLY provides for
    A. under-voltage protection
    B. short-circuit protection
    C. absorbing mechanical stresses or vibration when the device is closed
    D. delayed-time action

20. The PRIMARY importance of outrigging on a truck crane is
    A. to prevent the load from swinging
    B. to operate the bucket
    C. for lateral support of truck body
    D. to hold the boom in position

21. A shovel equipped with a dual crowd will MOST likely
    A. handle more cubic yards of material per hour
    B. require superior operators
    C. stall under harder digging
    D. have less tension in the crowd cable

22. The quotation "When an assembly is removed from a crane for replacement of a bushing, gear, or any individual part, it is an excellent practice to completely recondition the entire assembly."
Following the advice in this quotation, the Crane Engineman will MOST likely learn that
    A. it is cheaper to buy two or more different parts
    B. repetition of work on repairs can be eliminated
    C. replacement parts will wear less than original parts
    D. replacement of one part in an assembly is less costly in the long run

23. In reference to overhead traveling bucket cranes, the term dynamic braking means MOST NEARLY
    A. actuating a trustor brake
    B. energizing a magnetic type brake
    C. closing a magnetic contactor which permits the brake to close
    D. a method of reducing the speed of hoisting motors when lowering a load

24. The type of lubricant commonly used for a bridge motor gear case at low temperature (below 32°F.) is
    A. S.A.E.90   B. S.A.E. 160
    C. S.A.E.250   D. dip-gear grease

25. A gear-type transfer pump is one that USUALLY contains
    A. hydraulic plungers   B. rollers and pinions
    C. twin gear elements   D. poppet type valves

26. On a shovel boom the shipper shaft is USUALLY located near
    A. the top of the boom   B. the bottom of the boom
    C. the jack shaft drum   D. the mid-point of the boom

27. The characteristic of a series motor which makes its use desirable for cranes is that a large increase in torque is obtained
    A. with a large increase in voltage
    B. with a moderate increase in current
    C. when lowering a load
    D. with a moderate decrease in current

28. The compression ratio of a modern diesel engine has an approximate range of (with no starting ignition device)
    A. 3-5   B. 6-8   C. 9-11   D. 12-22

29. If you were to instruct an Oiler to do a sequence of jobs and operations, he would MOST likely do them
    A. in any order
    B. without regards to specifications
    C. when the machine is down
    D. in the prescribed order

30. The lifting ability of a crawler-mounted crane PRIMARILY
depends upon the
   A. gearing   B. engine power
   C. balance of the crane   D. strength of the cables

31. The breaking strength of a new 1/2" diameter 6 X 19 fiber
core wire rope made of plow steel is APPROXIMATELY
   A. 2 tons   B. 3 tons
   C. 5 tons   D. 10 tons

32. Of the following tools for cutting wire rope used on construc-
tion equipment, the one that is BEST is a(n)
   A. hacksaw   B. standard bolt cutter
   C. oxy-acetylene torch   D. cold chisel

33. The purpose of adding a jib boom to the regular boom of a
crane is to
   A. act as a counterweight when lifting
   B. prevent overloading
   C. shift the center of gravity
   D. obtain greater reach

34. When a crane is equipped with a jib boom, the lifting capacity
of the boom is APPROXIMATELY
   A. 1/2 of the crane load
   B. 3/4 of the crane load
   C. the same as the crane load
   D. 1 1/2 times the crane load

35. Of the following bell or whistle hoist signals, the one that
is customarily used to signal the lowering of a load is
   A. two quick signals   B. three quick signals
   C. one quick signal   D. a series of quick signals

36. An authorized signalman working in conjunction with the crane
operator has his arm extended, fingers clenched and thumb upward while moving his hand up and down. The signalman is sig-
nalling the crane operator to
   A. lift the boom up   B. lower the load
   C. hoist the load   D. stop immediately (Emergency)

Questions 37-40.

DIRECTIONS: The following four questions numbered 37 to 40 inclu-
            sive, are to be answered in accordance with the para-
            graph below:

   Operators spotting loads with long booms and working around men
need the smooth,easy operation and positive control of uniform pressure swing clutches. There are no jerks or grabs with these large
disc-type clutches because there is always even pressure over the
entire clutch lining surface. In the conventional band-type swing
clutch the pressure varies between dead and live ends of the band.
The uniform pressure swing clutch has excellent provision for heat
dissipation. The driving elements, which are always rotating, have
a great number of fins cast in them. This gives them an impeller
or blower action for cooling, resulting in longer life and freedom
from frequent adjustment.

37. According to the above paragraph, it may be said that conventional band-type swing clutches have
    A. even pressure on the clutch lining
    B. larger contact area
    C. smaller contact area
    D. uneven pressure on the clutch lining

38. According to the above paragraph, machines equipped with uniform pressure swing clutches will
    A. give better service under all conditions
    B. require no clutch adjustment
    C. give positive control of hoist
    D. provide better control of swing

39. According to the above paragraph, it may be said that the rotation of the driving elements of the uniform pressure swing clutch is always
    A. continuous   B. constant
    C. varying   D. uncertain

40. According to the above paragraph, freedom from frequent adjustment is due to the
    A. operator's smooth, easy operation
    B. positive control of the clutch
    C. cooling effect of the rotating fins
    D. larger contact area of the bigger clutch

KEY (CORRECT ANSWERS)

1.	B		21.	A
2.	D		22.	B
3.	C		23.	D
4.	A		24.	A
5.	C		25.	C
6.	C		26.	D
7.	A		27.	B
8.	B		28.	D
9.	D		29.	D
10.	A		30.	C
11.	B		31.	D
12.	C		32.	C
13.	C		33.	D
14.	B		34.	A
15.	A		35.	B
16.	D		36.	A
17.	B		37.	D
18.	A		38.	D
19.	D		39.	A
20.	C		40.	C

EXAMINATION SECTION

TEST 1

DIRECTIONS: Each question or incomplete statement is followed by several suggested answers or completions. Select the one that BEST answers the question or completes the statement. *PRINT THE LETTER OF THE CORRECT ANSWER IN THE SPACE AT THE RIGHT.*

1. When servicing a fleet of Cat D8 tractors, the PROPER method of refueling is to
   A. top off the tanks before each shift
   B. leave some room for expansion when filling at the start of each shift
   C. top off the tanks at the end of each shift
   D. use portable pumps for filling where possible

1.___

2. In order to PROPERLY install a flat metal lock, used with a cap screw, the lock should be bent
   A. in two 45-degree bends
   B. over a curved surface
   C. to catch the inside of the cap screw
   D. sharply on a flat surface of the cap screw

2.___

3. Bearings which require heat for installation should be heated in
   A. lubricating oil to 250°F   B. diesel fuel to 300°F
   C. lubricating oil to 400°F   D. diesel fuel to 400°F

3.___

4. A standard torque down test on a 1½" bolt, to be used with standard heat treated bolts and stud nuts in assembling Cat equipment, is _____ foot-lbs.
   A. 110 ± 115   B. 265 ± 50   C. 800 ± 400   D. 1500 ± 200

4.___

5. When assembling duo-cone floating seals in a Cat D8 tractor, the toric sealing ring SHOULD be assembled with
   A. a thumb and finger
   B. a torque wrench
   C. a 2000 PSI hydraulic press
   D. regular pliers and a screwdriver

5.___

6. When servicing the hydraulic system of a Cat D8 tractor and 8S bulldozer, the mechanic SHOULD put the control levers in the _____ position.
   A. hold   B. float   C. release   D. neutral

6.___

7. The one of the following conditions that would NOT be a possible direct cause of a Cat diesel engine in a crawler tractor overheating is
   A. low coolant level
   B. low fuel pressure
   C. corroded water pump
   D. leaking precombustion chamber gaskets

7.___

8. When a Cat D8 tractor water temperature regulator is being   8. ___
   checked for proper opening temperature, the regulator
   SHOULD start to open at
      A. 120°F   B. 144°F   C. 152°F   D. 164°F

9. In a Cat D8 tractor, the water pump is sealed with a   9. ___
   _____ seal.
      A. duo-cone   B. leather-faced bellows
      C. carbon-faced bellows   D. O-ring

10. The sealed pressure overflow assembly in a Cat D8 tractor's   10. ___
    radiator assembly has the PRIMARY purpose of
       A. maintaining a constant coolant level
       B. preventing air from entering
       C. preventing coolant from leaking out
       D. maintaining a constant pressure during tractor
          operation

11. The MAIN oil pump on a Cat D8 engine is driven by a   11. ___
       A. gear from the timing gear train
       B. belt from the fan belt assembly
       C. gear from the flywheel
       D. series of gears from the camshaft

12. The engine oil pump on a Cat D8 tractor is located in the   12. ___
    front section of the oil pan and can be worked on by
       A. removing the rear section of the oil pan
       B. removing the timing gear case
       C. removing the oil pan covers
       D. disassembling the bell housing

13. In the case of a Cat D8 power shift tractor transmission   13. ___
    failure, a CRITICAL requirement before returning the
    tractor to operation is to install a new
       A. engine oil cooler
       B. transmission oil cooler core assembly
       C. engine filter element
       D. transmission air cleaner

14. Valve rotation is a term which refers to the   14. ___
       A. removal and reassembly of all valves
       B. turn of the valves during engine operation
       C. placement of the valves in another location in the
          firing sequence
       D. normal tune-up procedure for the valves

15. The end gap in a newly-installed piston ring SHOULD be   15. ___
    measured with a _____ gage.
       A. feeler   B. ring   C. plug   D. surface

16. Pistons which have been removed from a diesel engine for   16. ___
    repair and replacement should be replaced IF
       A. they are scored above the top compressing ring
       B. the ring grooves are carboned up
       C. they are badly scored below the compressing ring
       D. the top ring is worn

17. When adjusting the alternator for proper voltage on a   17.___
newly-styled power-shift Cat D8 tractor, a mechanic SHOULD
use a(n)
    A. ammeter and a pair of pliers
    B. voltmeter and a socket wrench
    C. voltmeter and a screwdriver
    D. voltage regulator and a screwdriver

18. The one of the following phrases that does NOT accurately   18.___
describe the type of power-shift transmission in a 46A
power-shift Cat D8 tractor is
    A. planetary drive   B. oil actuated
    C. constant mesh   D. hydraulically engaged

19. When checking to insure proper PSI settings on the   19.___
steering clutch actuating pistons, the steering clutches
of a Cat D8 tractor SHOULD be
    A. *engaged* with the engine at full throttle
    B. *disengaged* with the engine at low idle
    C. *engaged* with the engine at low idle
    D. *disengaged* with the engine at full throttle

20. The hydraulic pump on the Cat D8 tractor power-shift   20.___
transmission supplies oil to the transmission
    A. only
    B. and torque converter only
    C. , torque converter, and steering clutches only
    D. , torque converter, steering clutches, and brakes

21. When the track on a Cat D8 tractor is being assembled,   21.___
the pad belts should have a torqued down pressure of
AT LEAST ____ PSI.
    A. 50 ± 10   B. 100 ± 20   C. 150 ± 30   D. 250 ± 50

22. The seals between the pin and bushings of the Cat D8   22.___
tractor are of the ____ type.
    A. bellows   B. O-ring
    C. duo-cone   D. leather-faced

23. As a safety measure, before removing the master pin on   23.___
the tracks of any track-type tractor, it is BEST to
    A. remove all pressure from the hydraulic track adjustor
    B. have the idler in the up position
    C. have the idler in the down position
    D. remove the duo-cone seals

24. When tracks on a Cat D8 are properly adjusted to minimize   24.___
wear, the sag between the carrier-roller and idler should
be NO MORE THAN
    A. ¼" to ½"   B. ½" to 1½"
    C. 1" to 1½"   D. 1½" to 2½"

25. To change the front idler on a tractor from the low to the   25.___
high position, a mechanic MUST rotate the
    A. bearing 180° only   B. bearing and idler 180°
    C. idler 180° only   D. shaft 180° only

26. The turbo-charger on any diesel engine performs the   26.___
    BASIC function of ____ air pressure.
    A. *decreasing* the intake   B. *increasing* the intake
    C. *decreasing* the exhaust   D. *increasing* the exhaust

27. The PRIMARY reason for removal of carbon from a turbine   27.___
    wheel of an automotive-type turbo-charger is to
    A. prevent hot spots
    B. prevent loss of air pressure
    C. increase manifold temperature
    D. prevent dynamic imbalance

28. If a timing gear has 120 teeth and turns at 700 RPM, the   28.___
    speed that a 420 tooth gear mated to it will turn at is
    ___ RPM.
    A. 150   B. 200   C. 500   D. 2450

29. The engine hydraulic system and transmission on a certain   29.___
    type of tractor use the same type oil. This oil is
    delivered in 55 gal. drums.
    How many drums are needed to make all three changes on
    ten of these tractors whose capacities are the following:
        Engine .... 58 quarts
        Transmission .... 70 quarts
        Hydraulic system ...... 22 gallons
    A. 100 drums   B. 50 drums
    C. 54 drums   D. 10 drums

30. A new shop layout requires the following: 30.___
            1,000 sq. ft. for tool room
            3,000 sq. ft. for parts room
           10,000 sq. ft. for service bays
            5,500 sq. ft. for isles
    The building should be AT LEAST ____ yards wide and
    ____ yards long.
    A. 10; 70   B. 20; 70   C. 25; 70   D. 30; 70

31. After moving a track-type tractor equipped with a bull-   31.___
    dozer into an area for servicing, the operator should
    ALWAYS
    A. lower the blade   B. ground the scarifier
    C. tilt the blade forward   D. lower the bowl

32. The diameter of the main journals on the crankshaft of a   32.___
    new series Cat D8 tractor is 4.259 to 4.261 inches.
    The MAXIMUM allowable main-bearing clearance should be
    no more than
    A. .003   B. .005   C. .007   D. .010

33. NORMAL procedure in removing the liners from a wet-type   33.___
    diesel engine would require the use of a
    A. puller ring and 4 lb. hammer
    B. brass puller rod and hammer
    C. manual puller
    D. hydraulic puller

34. When the crankshaft of a Cat D8 is worn sufficiently to require regrinding and standard oversized bearings are used, the shaft should be turned down to EITHER _____ undersize.
    A. .025" or .050"
    B. .010" or .020"
    C. .050" or 0.10"
    D. .001" or .002"

34. ___

35. To insure MAXIMUM cable life on a crawler-drawn scraper, the mechanic should
    A. grease the cable with engine oil
    B. replace the cable when any part is worn
    C. pull out a few feet of cable when worn
    D. grease the sheave grooves with gear lub

35. ___

36. PROPER procedure in filling a large earthmoving tire with air should include use of
    A. hand-held air lines
    B. steel hammers
    C. self-attaching air chucks
    D. chains and lifting hooks

36. ___

37. The bearing journals on a standard six-cylinder diesel engine with a four-stroke firing cycle are spaced _____ apart.
    A. 30°
    B. 60°
    C. 90°
    D. 120°

37. ___

38. The BASIC advantage of using an alternator over a generator on an automotive diesel engine is that the alternator
    A. provides alternating current
    B. provides full voltage at idle speeds
    C. provides better starting in cold weather
    D. is easier to adjust

38. ___

39. The normal SAE definition of net flywheel horsepower includes a requirement that the engine be running at rated RPM and that it be equipped with
    A. no attachments
    B. fan, generator and no water pump or radiator
    C. fan, generator, water pump and radiator
    D. fan, generator, water pump and no radiator

39. ___

40. GENERALLY, a diesel engine in a tractor or loader is operated with its compression ratio _____ as that of a gasoline engine.
    A. four times as great
    B. the same
    C. twice as great
    D. five times as great

40. ___

KEY (CORRECT ANSWERS)

1. C	11. A	21. D	31. A
2. D	12. C	22. C	32. C
3. A	13. B	23. A	33. D
4. D	14. B	24. C	34. A
5. A	15. A	25. B	35. C
6. A	16. A	26. B	36. C
7. B	17. C	27. D	37. B
8. D	18. C	28. B	38. B
9. C	19. B	29. D	39. C
10. D	20. D	30. D	40. C

TEST 2

Each question or incomplete statement is followed by several suggested answers or completions. Select the one that BEST answers the question or completes the statement. *PRINT THE LETTER OF THE CORRECT ANSWER IN THE SPACE AT THE RIGHT.*

1. In a normal automotive and earthmoving application, a STANDARD commercial diesel engine ignites the fuel at
    A. 450°F   B. 900°F   C. 1450°F   D. 212°F

1.___

2. The one of the following that is NOT normally used as a starting system for automotive and earthmoving diesel engines in mobile equipment is
    A. a gasoline starting engine
    B. a direct electric starting motor
    C. air pressure
    D. a hydraulic motor

2.___

3. A four-cycle diesel engine has a firing sequence BEST described as
    A. power, scavenging, compression, stroke, and firing
    B. intake, compression, firing, power, and exhaust
    C. exhaust, compression, firing, and power
    D. exhaust, intake, firing, and power

3.___

4. When a diesel engine is equipped with a gasoline starting engine, the compression release control is opened
    A. *after* the main engine is turning over
    B. *before* the main engine is turning over
    C. *after* the starting engine is at full RPM
    D. *after* the starting engine is turning the diesel engine

4.___

5. The one of the following that is NOT a normal method used to help start a diesel engine in cold weather is
    A. dip stick heaters   B. glow plugs
    C. manifold heating   D. ethylene glycol injection

5.___

6. The BASIC reason for cam grinding a diesel engine cylinder is so that
    A. the piston rings will seat better
    B. the piston will not stick in the lines
    C. it will become more nearly round when running hot
    D. it will not be as hard to turn over when starting

6.___

7. The turbo-charger used on a GM diesel engine is BEST described as ____ driven.
    A. exhaust-gas   B. intake-gas
    C. mechanically   D. hydraulically

7.___

8. When removing an 8S hydraulic bulldozer from a Cat D8   8.___
   tractor for tractor servicing, the bulldozer lift cylinders
   SHOULD be secured with
       A. hanger link, bolt, nut, and lockwasher
       B. master pin and link
       C. bracket and hose coupler
       D. J bolt clamps and pins

9. On an earthmoving machine, the hydraulic crossover valve   9.___
   has a function of being able to use
       A. two circuits with one valve
       B. one circuit with two valves
       C. both circuits at the same time
       D. varying pressures in the same circuit

10. When making adjustments on a clutch of a double-drum cable   10.___
    control mounted on a Cat D8 tractor used for pulling a
    scraper, a mechanic should ALWAYS
        A. disengage the clutch
        B. shut off the engine
        C. loosen the clamp nut and clutch-engaging nut lock bolt
        D. move the clutch-engaging rod one inch beyond the
           clutch engaged mark

11. The engine oil that should be used for a Cat D8 tractor   11.___
    using a Cat engine is
        A. superior lubricant Series 1
        B. superior lubricant Series 3
        C. standard multiviscosity Series 2
        D. standard multiviscosity Series 1

12. The engine oil that should be used for a Cummins diesel   12.___
    engine is
        A. superior lubricant Series 1
        B. superior lubricant Series 3
        C. standard multiviscosity Series 2
        D. standard multiviscosity Series 1

13. When the sulphur content of the diesel fuel used in a Cat   13.___
    diesel engine goes above 0.4%, the oil change period should
    be changed from ____ to ____ Service Meter Hours.
        A. 500; 300   B. 250; 125   C. 500; 100   D. 250; 100

14. In a four-stroke diesel engine, each piston fires every   14.___
    ____ of the crankshaft.
        A. revolution   B. 2 revolutions
        C. 4 revolutions   D. $\frac{1}{2}$ revolution

15. In an automotive engine, when the alternator is functioning 15.___
    properly and a low charging rate is experienced, the
    mechanic SHOULD check the
        A. magneto   B. generator
        C. regulator   D. battery cables

16. The PROPER equipment to use in removing a sprocket from   16.____
    a Cat D8 tractor is a
    A. hydraulic puller   B. chain hoist and fall
    C. socket wrench   D. bar and rubber hammer

17. The PROPER amount of pressure for installation of a Cat   17.____
    D8 sprocket on its splines is ____ to ____ tons.
    A. 10; 20   B. 20; 25   C. 35; 40   D. 60; 65

18. Segmented sprocket teeth on a tractor makes it EASIER to   18.____
    A. make pin contact   B. make bushing contact
    C. clean the tracks   D. assemble the tracks

19. The one of the following that is NOT an OSHA requirement   19.____
    while working on heavy construction machinery is wearing
    A. safety glasses   B. safety shoes
    C. a hard hat   D. loose clothing

20. The one of the following that is the BEST way to store   20.____
    oily rags is
    A. in a closed metal container
    B. piled in a corner of the repair shop
    C. in a covered wooden box
    D. piled under a work bench

21. The reason for NOT going to full throttle immediately   21.____
    when starting a turbo-charged automotive-type diesel
    engine is to
    A. allow the bearings to warm up
    B. prevent the engine oil from diluting
    C. ensure bearing lubrication
    D. ensure equal heating of the turbine blades

22. A Cummins diesel engine model designated as NTA-370 is   22.____
    BEST described as
    A. naturally aspirated, torque adjusted, and 370 max.
       horsepower
    B. four valve head, turbo-charged, after cooled, and
       370 max. horsepower
    C. naturally aspirated, turbo-charged, after cooled,
       and 370 max. horsepower
    D. 16 valve turbo-charged intercooled and 370 max. horsepower

23. Of the following phrases, the one that does NOT describe   23.____
    a common arrangement common in a V-type automotive diesel
    engine is
    A. two cam shafts   B. two timing gear trains
    C. one crankshaft   D. two exhaust manifolds

24. The normal oil temperature range for a Cummins diesel   24.____
    engine is MOST NEARLY
    A. 140 to 160°F   B. 140 to 220°F
    C. 180 to 290°F   D. 180 to 225°F

25. The one of the following that is NOT a safety requirement   25.____
    when using ether as a cold weather starting aid on a diesel
    engine is never
       A. spray directly into the manifold
       B. use near an open flame
       C. use with a preheater
       D. use with a flame-thrower

Questions 26-28.

DIRECTIONS: Questions 26 through 28, inclusive, are to be answered
               in accordance with the following paragraph.

   *The following is a set of instructions on engine shut-down
procedure: When an engine equipped with an electric shut-down
valve is used, the engine can be shut down completely by turning
off the switch key on installations equipped with an electric shut-
down valve, or by turning the manual shut-down valve lever. Turning
off the switch key which controls the electric shut-down valve
always stops the engine unless the override button on the shut-down
valve has been locked in the open position. If the manual override
on the electric shut-down valve is being used, turn the button full
counterclockwise to stop the engine.*

*CAUTION: Never leave the switch key or the override button in the
valve open or run position when the engine is not running. With
overhead tanks, this would allow fuel to drain into the cylinder,
causing hydraulic lock.*

26. According to the above paragraph, it becomes apparent that   26.____
    if an engine does not stop when the electric shut-down
    valve switch key is shut off,
       A. an open manual switch is present
       B. the override button is locked in the closed position
       C. a closed manual switch is functioning
       D. the override button is locked in the open position

27. When using an engine equipped with an electric shut-down   27.____
    valve,
       A. no alternate method is available
       B. a manual method is not present
       C. a manual override can shut the engine down
       D. a manual override will not work

28. As a matter of caution, the switch key in the closed   28.____
    position or the override button in the stop position will
       A. assist in keeping fuel in the cylinders
       B. prevent fuel from flooding the cylinder cavities
       C. assist in producing hydraulic lock
       D. aid fuel dilution

29. A detroit diesel engine with the designation of 8V-53N is   29.____
    BEST described as an ____ with a cubic inch displacement
    of ____ cu. in.
       A. 8 cylinder V-type; 212   B. 16 cylinder V-type; 424
       C. 8 cylinder N-type; 848   D. 8 cylinder V-type; 424

30. Diesel engine fuels are rated by number from 1 to 4.   30.___
The relationship between the flash point of a fuel and
its number is that, as the flash point
   A. *increases*, the numbers either increase or decrease,
      depending on the volatility of the fuel
   B. *increases*, the numbers increase
   C. *decreases*, the numbers increase
   D. *decreases*, the numbers decrease

31. In order to locate a misfiring cylinder in a GM diesel   31.___
engine, the valve cover should be removed and each
cylinder checked by
   A. holding down the injector follower
   B. using a pressure gage
   C. regapping the plugs
   D. increasing the fuel to each cylinder one at a time

32. When a GM diesel engine is being serviced, the NORMAL   32.___
interval for cleaning the cooling system is ____ hours
or _____ miles.
   A. 200; 600   B. 500; 15,000
   C. 1000; 30,000   D. 1500; 60,000

33. The one of the following situations that will NOT cause 33.___
the automatic electrical shut-down system on a GM engine
to stop the engine is
   A. a loss of coolant   B. a loss of oil pressure
   C. overspeeding   D. a decrease in R.P.M.

34. A medium range thermostat for a Cummins diesel engine   34.___
NORMALLY has a range of
   A. 170 to 185°F   B. 140 to 160°F
   C. 180 to 195°F   D. 120 to 145°F

35. When filling a diesel engine cooling system, the mix   35.___
required is 80% antifreeze and 20% water. You are required
to fill seven systems containing 30 gals. each.
The number of 5 gal. cans of antifreeze that are required
is MOST NEARLY
   A. 210   B. 168   C. 34   D. 26

36. When changing a *throw-away* type fuel filter element on a   36.___
Cummins diesel engine, the housing should be tightened
   A. with a torque wrench
   B. with a socket wrench
   C. with a hand clamp and a screwdriver
   D. by hand

37. Hydraulic hoses are NORMALLY rated by ____ rating.   37.___
   A. cord ply   B. stul mesh
   C. P.S.I.   D. C.F.M.

38. The starting system of a diesel engine is actuated by   38.___
2-12 volt batteries in parallel.
The electric current produced is ____ volt ____.
   A. 12; D.C.   B. 24; D.C.   C. 12; A.C.   D. 24; A.C.

39. Fan belt checks and adjustments, using the suggested   39. ___
    A,B,C Cummins maintenance manual method, are FIRST
    required at the ___ interval.
    A. A   B. B   C. C   D. D

40. When two 12-volt 450-ampere-hour batteries are installed   40. ___
    in series, the system is rated as ___ volt-___ Amp hour.
    A. 24; 450   B. 12; 900   C. 12; 450   D. 24; 900

KEY (CORRECT ANSWERS)

1. C	11. B	21. C	31. A
2. D	12. A	22. B	32. C
3. B	13. B	23. B	33. D
4. B	14. B	24. D	34. A
5. D	15. C	25. A	35. C
6. C	16. A	26. D	36. D
7. C	17. D	27. C	37. C
8. A	18. D	28. B	38. A
9. A	19. D	29. D	39. B
10. B	20. A	30. B	40. A

EXAMINATION SECTION
TEST 1

DIRECTIONS: Answer the following questions directly, briefly, and succinctly.

QUESTIONS

1. How does the manner in which fuel and air are admitted to the cylinders of Diesel and gasoline engines differ?

2. In a Diesel engine, how is the heat required for ignition generated?

3. If a Diesel engine and a gasoline engine each have a compression ratio at the upper limit, which engine will develop the greater pressure during the compression event?

4. Why is energy from an external source necessary for ignition in a gasoline engine?

5. What is the relationship between the pressure in the cylinder after the compression event and the power output of an engine?

6. What determines the highest practical compression ratio for a gasoline engine?

7. List *three* factors which determine when ignition should occur.

8. Is maximum power developed in the cylinder of an engine before or after the piston reaches TDC?

9. Does the time required for combustion vary with engine speed?

10. Why is the pressure developed in the cylinder of a gasoline engine less when ignition occurs later than when it occurs at the normal ignition time?

11. How is fuel related to the maximum-combustion pressure developed in the cylinder of a Diesel engine?

12. With respect to Diesel engines, what is meant by turbulence?

13. Why is turbulence necessary in a cylinder of a Diesel engine?

14. Which *two* parts of a combustion space may include design features which aid in creating turbulence?

15. What is the principal constructional difference between an open combustion chamber and other types?

16. With respect to Diesel engines, what is precombustion?

17. Why is precombustion used in some engines?

18. In engines equipped with precombustion chambers, where is the major portion of the injected fuel burned?

19. Which characteristic of gasoline determines how much fuel will be vaporized?

20. What is meant by vapor lock?

21. In addition to difficulty in starting the engine, name *two* troubles which may occur if the gasoline is not completely vaporized when it enters the combustion space.

22. Name *two* symptoms of detonation which occur during engine operation.

23. With respect to the phases of combustion, when will detonation occur in a gasoline engine; in a Diesel engine?

24. In general, what causes detonation in a gasoline engine?

25. What is the principal factor which determines the octane rating of a fuel required for a given engine?

26. In a Diesel engine, what is meant by ignition delay?

27. In addition to the characteristics of the fuel, which factors determine the duration of ignition delay in a Diesel engine?

28. Are fuels with a low or high volatility most desirable for Diesel engines?

———

KEY (CORRECT ANSWERS)

1. Fuel and air are admitted separately to the cylinders of a Diesel engine; and as a mixture to the cylinders of a gasoline engine.

2. By compression of intake air.

3. Diesel.

4. Because the heat caused by compression is not great enough to cause self-ignition of the combustible mixture.

5. The higher the pressure, the greater the power output.

6. The characteristics of the fuel used.

7. Engine speed, type of fuel, and compression ratio.

8. After.

9. No.

10. Because combustion takes place in larger space.

11. The rate and amount of fuel injected determine maximum pressure.

12. Motion of air within the combustion space.

13. To bring sufficient air in contact with injected fuel particles to ensure complete combustion.

14. Piston crown and cylinder head.

15. Open chambers have no auxiliary combustion chambers.

16. The conditioning of all or part of the fuel, by partial burning, before it enters the main combustion space.

17. To aid in creating the turbulence necessary for the proper mixing of air and fuel.

18. Main combustion space.

19. Volatility.

20. The formation of vapors in the fuel system which block or restrict the flow of fuel to the carburetor.

21. Improper fuel distribution and crankcase dilution.

22. Loss of power and undesirable combustion noises.

23. During the final phase; start of second phase.

24. Anything which increases excessively the temperature or pressure of the unburned mixture in the combustion space.

25. Compression ratio.

26. The interval of time between the injection and the ignition of fuel.

27. The temperature and pressure of the compressed air in the combustion space, the average size of the injected fuel particles, and the amount of turbulence in the combustion space.

28. Fuels with a low volatility.

———

TEST 2

QUESTIONS

1.   What is the *BASIC* difference between the two common types of
spark-ignition systems?

2.   What is the *PRIMARY* purpose of the battery in a spark-ignition
system?

3.   What is the purpose of the shell of laminated iron that usually
encloses the windings of an ignition coil?

4.   What is the *BASIS* for sometimes calling the ignition coil of a
battery-ignition system an induction coil?

5.   What is the *PURPOSE* of the breaker assembly in an ignition
system?

6.   In what *two* ways may the two-coil, double-breaker assembly
arrangement be used in an ignition system?

7.   What happens to the voltage in the primary circuit of an ignition system when a high voltage is induced in the secondary
winding of an ignition coil?

8.   Which part of an ignition system functions to prevent arcing
across the breaker-assembly points as they open?

9.   What are the *two PRINCIPAL* parts of an ignition system distributing mechanism?

10.   What is the *FUNCTION* of the rotating part of a distributing
mechanism?

11.   Why are the distributor rotor and the breaker-assembly cam
driven at one-half engine speed?

12.   What causes the points of a breaker assembly to open and
close?

13.   If the breaker assembly is moved a few degrees in a direction
opposite to the direction of cam rotation, is the time of
spark occurrence, with respect to piston position, retarded
or advanced?

14.   If the time of spark occurrence is changed by moving the
breaker-assembly cam, will moving the cam in a direction
opposite to the direction of rotation retard or advance the
spark?

15.   Which forces are utilized to operate automatic spark-control
devices so that the time of spark is advanced?

16.   When engine speed decreases, what causes an automatic spark-
control mechanism to retard the spark?

17. Which type of automatic control mechanism is used when variations in the timing of the spark are governed by engine speed?

18. Why are centrifugal and vacuum-type spark-control mechanisms sometimes used in combination?

19. The force which causes a distributor to move from the retarded position is transmitted from which part in a vacuum spark-control mechanism?

20. When a vacuum spark-control mechanism is in the retarded position, will the opening of the passage to the control unit be on the carburetor side or the manifold side of the throttle valve?

21. What is the *PRINCIPAL* difference between the *two* common types of spark plugs?

22. What determines the extent to which a spark plug will dissipate heat?

23. How do the metal housings or braided metal casings sometimes used to enclose the components of an ignition system prevent electrical interference in radio receiving equipment?

24. On the basis of the manner in which electromagnetic induction may be produced in a magneto, what are the *two* types of magnetos?

25. Is a separate ignition coil *NECESSARY* with a magneto which generates high voltage?

26. Is the distributing mechanism of a low-voltage magneto-ignition system located in the primary circuit or in the secondary circuit?

27. With respect to circuits, how does the location of the distributing mechanism in a low-voltage magneto-ignition system *differ from* the location of this mechanism in other types of ignition systems?

28. List *three* advantages which a low-voltage magneto-ignition system has over a magneto system of the high-voltage type?

29. If a magneto does not generate the high voltage required for ignition when an engine is being started, how is the necessary voltage obtained during the cranking interval?

30. Does the current from the booster coil flow through the magneto?

31. What is the difference in the manner by which ignition-over-speed safety devices function to control speed in battery-ignition and magneto-ignition systems?

KEY (CORRECT ANSWERS)

1. The source of electrical energy.

2. To energize the secondary, or high-voltage, winding of the ignition coil.

3. To serve as a conductor for the magnetic field.

4. The coil operates on the principle of electromagnetic induction; in other words, the coil depends on the inductive effect of the magnetism produced by the low voltage in the primary winding to produce high voltage in the secondary winding.

5. To act as a switch, opening and closing the primary circuit.

6. To provide a single spark to each cylinder; and to provide two sparks simultaneously to each cylinder.

7. It is momentarily increased because a voltage is also induced in the primary circuit when the breaker points open and the magnetic field collapses.

8. The condenser.

9. Rotor (distributing arm) and cap (head).

10. To close the secondary circuit, so that current from a high-voltage side of the coil will flow to the proper spark plug.

11. So that half of the spark plugs will fire during each revolution of the crankshaft.

12. Lobes on the breaker-assembly cam.

13. Advanced.

14. Retard.

15. Centrifugal force and vacuum.

16. The action of springs.

17. Centrifugal.

18. So that proper spark-control is provided under all conditions of speed and load.

19. Spring-loaded diaphragm.

20. On the carburetor side.

21. The material used in the insulator or core.

22. The amount of insulator exposed to the combustion gases.

23. By absorbing and grounding the high-frequency current given off by the parts of the ignition system.

24. Armature wound and inductor type.

25. No.

26. In the primary circuit.

27. In the low-voltage magneto system, the distributing mechanism
    is located in the primary circuit; and it is located in the
    secondary circuit in the battery-ignition and high-voltage
    magneto-ignition systems.

28. Shorter high-voltage leads, less electrical loss, and problems
    of a less serious nature in insulation and shielding.

29. Either from a booster coil-and-battery circuit or from the
    magneto by increasing its speed with an impulse mechanism.

30. No.

31. In a battery ignition system, the safety device opens the pri-
    mary circuit to stop the flow of current; in a magneto-ignition
    system, the primary circuit is grounded.

———

TEST 3

DIRECTIONS: Answer the following questions directly, briefly, and
succinctly.

QUESTIONS

1. Name *four* functions of an engine lubricating oil.

2. How does lubricating oil reduce friction between bearing surfaces?

3. In addition to reducing friction, why is an oil seal necessary
between the piston rings and the cylinder wall?

4. What are the *PRINCIPAL* engine parts which lubricating oil may
cool?

5. With respect to the engine, where may the heat absorbed by
lubricating oil be dissipated?

6. The thickness of the oil film between two bearing surfaces is
determined *PRINCIPALLY* by which property of the oil?

7. Which characteristics of an engine determine the viscosity of
the lubricating oil to be used?

8. What is meant by the detergent power of an oil?

9. What is the purpose of the symbol numbers assigned to oils?

10. How are the lubricating qualities of an oil *IMPROVED* by
chemical additives?

11. If the recommended compounded oil is not available in sufficient quantities, would it be *better* to use a straight mineral
oil or a mixture of additive- and mineral-type oils?

12. What is the *most likely* source of trouble if corrosion is found
on the internal surfaces of an engine which uses compounded oil?

13. Does the suspension of fine particles of gummy material and
carbon in an additive-type oil indicate a reduction in the
lubricating quality of the oil?

14. In a centrifugal purifier, what causes sediment, water, and
oil to form separate layers?

15. In brief, what is the purification process when a purifier is
used as a separator? As a clarifier?

16. What determines whether a purifier should be used as a separator
or as a clarifier?

17. Is the principle of operation or the design of the rotating
elements the *principal* difference between the two common types
of purifiers?

18. In which type of purifier does the oil enter and leave through the top of the bowl?

19. What is the purpose of the three-wing device in the bowl of a tubular type purifier?

20. When should a purifier be operated at *less than* rated capacity?

21. When a purifier is used as a separator, what will be the result if the bowl is *NOT* primed with water?

22. What is the *PRINCIPAL* factor determining the length of time required to purify a lubricating oil?

23. Should the pressure or the temperature of the oil admitted to a purifier be increased in order to facilitate purification?

24. What is the result if the pressure on the oil admitted to a purifier is reduced? *Why?*

25. What determines the size of the discharge ring to be used for the purification of a given oil?

26. How can the general efficiency of a purifier be determined if an analysis of the purified oil cannot be made?

27. What type of chemical compound is included in a grease which is to be used where operating temperatures and loads are not excessive but where moisture is present?

28. Why is graphite grease *NOT* recommended as a lubricant for ball bearings or roller bearings?

———

KEY (CORRECT ANSWERS)

1. To prevent metal-to-metal contact; to form a seal between the piston rings and the cylinder; to aid in engine cooling; and to aid in preventing and removing sludge formations.

2. By forming a film which prevents direct contact between moving metal surfaces.

3. To prevent blow-by of gases.

4. Bearings, journals, and pistons.

5. To the mass of oil in the sump or to the water in the cooling system.

6. Viscosity.

7. Operating temperatures, speeds, pressures, and bearing clearances.

8. The oil's ability to remove or to prevent the accumulation of carbon deposits.

9. To identify the use and viscosity of each oil.

10. The tendency of the oil to stick to metal surfaces and the natural detergent property of the oil are improved by additives; additives also inhibit oxidation.

11. A mixture of additive- and mineral-type oils.

12. Water or partially burned fuel in the lubricating oil.

13. No.

14. The difference in the specific gravities of the sediment, water, and oil.

15. When used as a separator, the purifier separates oil from water and sediment. When used as a clarifier, a purifier separates oil from sediment only.

16. The moisture content of the oil being purified.

17. The design of the rotating elements.

18. Disk type.

19. To rotate the oil at the speed at which the bowl is rotating.

20. When it is being used as a separator with 9000 series oil.

21. Oil will be lost though the water-discharge ports.

22. The viscosity of the oil.

23. Temperature.

24. Purification is improved, because the reduction in the pressure increases the length of time the oil is subjected to centrifugal force.

25. The specific gravity of the oil.

26. By observing the clarity of the purified oil and the amount of oil in the separated water.

27. A lime-soap.

28. Because of its abrasive characteristic.

———

TEST 4

DIRECTIONS: Answer the following questions directly, briefly, and succinctly.

QUESTIONS

1. Which type of pump is used in engine lubricating-oil systems?

2. Name *two* types of pressure-control devices that may be incorporated in a lubricating-oil pump.

3. How does a control device regulate lubricating-oil pressure?

4. Why are *two* elements included in some lubricating-oil strainers?

5. Is oil flow to the engine stopped when a simplex strainer becomes clogged? *Why?*

6. Name *two* types of elements that are used in metal-edge type strainers.

7. How is the element of a metal-edge type strainer cleaned, without connections being broken or the flow of oil being interrupted?

8. Screen-type strainers are usually located on which side of the pressure pump?

9. Why is Fuller's earth *NOT* permitted in filters approved for use in engine lubricating-oil systems?

10. Name *three* types of lubricating-oil filtering systems.

11. In which type of lubricating-oil filtering system does all of the oil discharged by the pump flow directly to the engine through a strainer, a filter, and a cooler?

12. How does a sump-type filtering system *differ from* a shunt-type system?

13. With which type lubricating-oil-filtering system is it possible to filter the oil when the engine is not operating?

14. In a lubricating-oil system in which the filtering system is of the sump type, what is the path of oil from the oil supply to the engine inlet? (Indicate path by listing main components in the proper order.)

15. Name the *two* types of filtering systems in which oil flows directly from the filter back to the sump.

16. What *LIMITS* the amount of oil which flows through the filter of a bypass-type filtering system?

17. By listing the main parts of the system in their proper order, trace the path of oil through the external section of a lubricating-oil system which includes a shunt-type filtering system.

18. Name *two* ways in which oil for cooling may be supplied to the pistons of an engine.

19. What is the *FIRST* part to which lubricating oil usually flows after it enters the engine?

20. When is use made of the auxiliary pump which is incorporated in some lubricating systems?

21. How is oil supplied to the crankpin bearings, in most engines?

22. How are the crankshaft bearings lubricated in small gasoline engines which have no lubricating oil system?

23. List *four* UNDESIRABLE conditions which may occur if the crankcase of an engine is not properly ventilated.

24. In gasoline engines, unburned fuel may blow-by the compression rings, enter the crankcase, and dilute the lubricating oil. This situation is less likely to occur in a 2-stroke cycle engine. *Why?*

25. How are oil particles sometimes prevented from entering the blowers of engines in which the crankcase is ventilated to the intake system?

26. What happens to the harmful vapors which are vented from the crankcase to the intake system?

27. How may a crankshaft-bearing failure lead to a crankcase explosion?

28. What is the *BEST* source of information when you are checking an operating engine for symptoms of an impending bearing failure?

29. Why will fuel-diluted lubricating oil contribute *more readily* to conditions which may cause a crankcase explosion, than will oil which is not diluted by fuel?

———

KEY (CORRECT ANSWERS)

1. Positive-displacement rotary-gear pump.

2. Pressure-regulating valve; pressure-relief valve.

3. By recirculating excess oil from the pump discharge back to the pump intake or by discharging the excess oil directly to the oil sump.

4. In order that one element can be bypassed and removed for cleaning without interruption to the flow of oil to the engine.

5. No, because strainers of this type are provided with pressure-relief valves through which all oil may be bypassed to the engine.

6. Edge-wound metal ribbon; edge-type disks.

7. By manual rotation of the element against metallic scrapers, which remove the material caught by the element.

8. On the suction, or intake, side.

9. Fuller's earth removes the compounds (detergents) from additive-type oils.

10. Shunt, sump, and bypass.

11. Shunt.

12. In a sump-type filtering system, the filter is placed in a separate system in which oil is circulated by a motor-driven pump; the filter in a shunt-type system is located in the main lubricating-oil system.

13. Sump-type filtering system.

14. Sump, pump, cooler, and strainer.

15. Sump-type and bypass-type.

16. The size of the piping, and an orifice.

17. Sump tank, pump, strainer, filter, and cooler.

18. (a) Through drilled passages in the connecting rod.
    (b) By nozzles connected to an oil manifold.

19. Manifold (also called galley, or header).

20. An auxiliary pump is used if the lubricating-oil pump fails; it may also be used to circulate oil through the system when the engine is not operating.

21. Crankpin bearings usually receive oil from the main bearings, through drilled passages in the crankshaft.

22. By oil, mixed with the gasoline, which enters the engine with the fuel-air mixture.

23. An explosive mixture may accumulate; the lubricating oil may be diluted; corrosion may take place within the crankcase; and the lubricating oil may become emulsified.

24. Because the unburned fuel which might blow-by the compression rings is trapped in the intake ports and is forced back into the combustion space by the scavenging air when the intake ports are uncovered by the piston.

25. By the fine-wire screen device which separates the oil from the ventilating air and causes the oil to drain back to the oil supply.

26. They are forced into the combustion space and are either burned or discharged with the exhaust.

27. By causing excess heat, which vaporizes the oil; and by causing sparks, which may ignite the explosive mixture.

28. The oil pressure gage.

29. Because the flash point of the fuel is lower than that of lubricating oil, fuel-diluted oil tends to form an explosive mixture more rapidly than does lubricating oil, which is not diluted.

———

TEST 5

QUESTIONS

1. List *three* reasons why the temperature of an engine *MUST NOT*
be allowed to exceed a specified limit.

2. How may excessive heat in an engine affect lubrication?

3. How may too low an engine temperature affect the lubricating
oil and the cylinders of an engine?

4. How may inadequate engine cooling cause a wrist pin to seize?

5. Trace the path which water follows in a typical open cooling
system, by listing the various parts and passages in the proper
order.

6. Does the water flow through the exhaust-silencer water jacket
after passing through the engine in all open cooling systems?

7. In engines equipped with open cooling systems, what are *two*
possible sources of the heat that is used to raise the temperature of engine intake water?

8. In a closed cooling system, how is salt-water cooling of the
fresh water accomplished if there is no separate sea-water
circuit?

9. Starting with the discharge side of the fresh-water pump, trace
the path of water through the fresh-water circuit of a cooling
system by listing the parts and passages in the proper order.

10. Trace the path of water through the sea-water circuit of a
closed cooling system by listing the parts and passages in the
proper order.

11. Why is an auxiliary, or detached, pump provided in the cooling
systems of some engines?

12. Name *three* ways in which the fresh- and sea-water pumps of a
cooling system may differ.

13. Name *three* types of pumps which are used in engine cooling
systems.

14. Of the three types of pumps used in engine cooling systems,
which is the *most common?*

15. Name *three* methods by which tee pumps of a cooling system may
be driven.

16. Name *three* fluids, essential to engine operation, the temperatures of which are maintained at proper operating levels by
coolers.

17. Coolers, as used in the cooling systems of engines, may be of which *three* types?

18. Name the *two PRINCIPAL* parts of a shell-and-tube cooler.

19. Describe briefly the paths which the cooling and cooled liquids generally take through a shell-and-tube cooler.

20. In a shell-and-tube cooler, why is one of the tube sheets so arranged that it "floats" within the shell?

21. What is meant by the term *counterflow* when it is used to describe a type of shell-and-tube cooler?

22. Is a strut-tube cooler *larger* or *smaller* than a shell-and-tube cooler which provides the same amount of heat transfer?

23. If a strut-tube cooler and a shell-and-tube cooler provide an equal amount of heat transfer, which will withstand a *HIGHER* degree of scaling and larger foreign particles without clogging the cooling system?

24. Name *three* functions served by the "struts" in a strut-tube water cooler.

25. Of the three types of coolers used in engine cooling systems, which one is used *only* for the cooling of lubricating oil?

26. What is a "hull" cooler?

27. Which devices are installed in the salt-water circuit of an engine cooling system to protect the circuit from corrosion caused by electrolysis?

28. Do the devices which are installed to protect the sea-water circuit from corrosion prevent galvanic action?

29. Which terms are used to distinguish between the forms, or types, of zincs?

30. Which of the engine cooling passages which are common to in-line and V-type engines are not found in engines of the opposed-piston type?

31. Indicate how the paths of water through the GM 16-278A and FM 38D differ, by listing, in the order of flow, the parts and passages for each engine (start and end with the pump).

32. What is the *PURPOSE* of the tank that is provided in the fresh-water circuit of an engine cooling system?

———

KEY (CORRECT ANSWERS)

1. To maintain adequate lubrication; to prevent excessive variations in dimensions of parts; and to retain strength of metals.

2. Excess heat may reduce viscosity to a point where the oil film between parts may be destroyed. Also, heat causes oxidation of the oil and the formation of sludge.

3. An excessively low engine temperature may: cause corrosive gases to condense on the cylinder walls; increase ignition lag, causing detonation; and cause condensation, which leads to the formation of acid and sludge in the lubricating oil.

4. Inadequate cooling may allow an engine to overheat to the extent that closely fitted parts will seize because of the expansion of parts and the reduction of clearance.

5. Sea chest or scoop, strainer, sea valves, pump, lubricating-oil cooler, engine passages and jackets, exhaust-silencer water jackets, and overboard outlet.

6. No.

7. Lubricating oil and exhaust gases.

8. The fresh-water cooler is located outside of the hull, below the water line, in direct contact with the sea water.

9. Pump (discharge), engine passages, fresh-water cooler, lubricating-oil cooler (when applicable), and pump (suction).

10. Sea chest, strainer, sea valves, fresh-water cooler, lubricating-oil cooler (when applicable), exhaust cooling passages, and overboard outlets.

11. To be used in the event of attached-pump failure and to provide a means of cooling after the engine has been secured.

12. Fresh- and sea-water pumps may differ in type, size, and capacity.

13. Centrifugal, gear, and rotary (vane).

14. Centrifugal.

15. Gears, pulley and V-belt, and coupling.

16. Fresh water, lubricating oil, and air (in some cases).

17. Shell-and-tube, strut-tube, and plate-tube.

18. The tube bundle (bank, nest) and the shell.

19. The cooled liquid generally flows through the tubes; the cooling liquid generally flows around the tubes.

20. To allow for expansion of the tube bundle.

21. That the direction of liquid flow in the tubes is opposite to that in the shell.

22. Smaller.

23. The shell-and-tube cooler.

24. "Struts" increase the inside and outside contact surfaces of the tube, create turbulence in the liquid flowing through the tube, and increase the structural strength of the tube.

25. Plate-tube cooler.

26. A fresh-water cooler which is located outside the hull, below the water line, in direct contact with the sea water.

27. Zincs.

28. No. Zincs are installed to provide a replaceable surface for the attach of galvanic action.

29. Pencil and plate.

30. Cylinder-head passages.

31. GM 16-278A: Pump, water manifold, liner passages, head passages, exhaust passages, cooler, and pump.
    FM 38D: Pump, exhaust passages, liner passages, water header, cooler, pump.

32. The tank provides a place where water may be added to the system, and a space to accommodate variations in the volume of the water.

———

EXAMINATION SECTION
TEST 1

DIRECTIONS: Answer the following questions directly, briefly, and
succinctly.

QUESTIONS

1. When a gear train is designed to increase the torque on the
    driven shaft, will the larger gear be the driving gear or
    the driven gear?

2. When a drive mechanism is designed so that the torque of the
    shaft of the driven unit is three times that of the shaft of
    the driving unit, what is the speed of the driven unit, com-
    pared to that of the driving unit?

3. What is the speed ratio of a gear train in which the driving
    gear has 24 teeth and the driven gear has 48 teeth?

4. Does the preceding example represent an increase or a decrease
    in the speed of the driven gear, compared to the speed of the
    driving gear?

5. Will a drive mechanism increase power?

6. State the *three-fold* purpose of an indirect-type, mechanical,
    drive mechanism.

7. Why are reduction gears necessary in the propulsion units of
    some vessels?

8. Give *two* methods by which the direction of rotation of the
    propeller may be reversed in mechanical-drive propulsion units.

9. Mechanical connections exist between all but which two major
    components of the propulsion plant in a Diesel-electric-driven
    vessel?

10. Most Diesel-electric drives operate on which type of current?

11. How is astern operation accomplished with an electric drive?

12. When a reduction gear is installed in a Diesel-electric drive,
    is the reduction gear located
    (a) between the engine and the generator,
    (b) between the generator and the motor, or
    (c) between the motor and the propeller?

13. State *two* advantages that a flexible-type coupling has over a
    solid-type coupling.

14. From which *two* sources may oil for the lubrication of gear
    assemblies in an indirect-drive mechanism be supplied?

15. State *two* ways in which oil may be returned from a transmission
    to the engine lubricating-oil system.

16. What is indicated by an overflow of foaming oil from the vent
    of a reduction-gear case?

KEY (CORRECT ANSWERS)

1. The driven gear.

2. The speed of the driven unit is one-third that of the driving unit.

3. 2/1.

4. Decrease.

5. No.

6. (a) To reduce or increase the shaft speed of the driven unit, compared to the speed of the driving unit;
   (b) to provide a means of reversing the direction of rotation of the driven shaft; and
   (c) to permit quick-disconnect ot the driving unit and the driven unit.

7. To reduce propeller speed to the most efficient operating level.

8. By reversing the direction of engine operation; and by the use of reverse gears.

9. The generator and the motor.

10. Direct.

11. By reversing the flow of current to the motor, which, in turn, reverses the direction of rotation of the rotor to the motor and of the propeller.

12. (c) Between the motor and the propeller.

13. Flexible couplings absorb vibration and permit some misalignment of the driving and driven units.

14. The engine lubricating-oil system; an independent oil-system.

15. By gravity; by a scavenging system.

16. That the oil level in the gear case is too high.

TEST 2

DIRECTIONS: Answer the following questions directly, briefly, and succinctly.

QUESTIONS

1. With respect to engine lubrication, what is required when the jacking gear of a diesel engine is being used?

2. How are special devices used to aid in starting diesel engines in cold weather?

3. On the basis of the source of heat, name *two* types of air-intake heaters.

4. Which fluid is generally used as an auxiliary fuel in starting diesel engines in cold weather?

5. Give *two* reasons why engine parts may be damaged if load is applied too suddenly to a diesel engine which has not reached normal, operating temperatures.

6. Name *two* conditions, in addition to damage to engine parts, which may occur if a deisel engine is operated for a long period of time at less than 30 percent power.

7. Name *three* symptoms which indicate that an engine is overloaded.

8. List *five* lubricating checks, or operations, which may be required during diesel-engine operation.

9. Identify the diesel-engine systems to which the following operating temperature ranges apply:
   (1) 100° -130°F ;   (2) 140° -170°F ;   (3) 140° -180°F.

10. Give *two* methods by which the temperature of engine cooling-water may be controlled.

11. When an automatic temperature-regulator is installed in the sea-water circuit of an engine cooling system, where is the bulb of the temperature-control element located?

12. To what does the term "critical speed" apply?

13. Why should an overspeed safety device be tripped when a diesel engine is being stopped after normal operation?

14. After a diesel engine is stopped, what is sometimes done to accelerate the cooling of the engine?

15. What should be done if the relief valve on a cylinder of an operating diesel engine lifts several times?

16. What precaution must be taken to ensure that an explosion will not occur when the gasoline-engine power plant of a boat is started?

17. Why does the bayonet gage in the lubricating-oil systems of some engines have two scribed marks?

18. If fuel for the gasoline-engine power-plant of a boat is available from two wing tanks and a center tank, which tank should be selected as a source of fuel when the power plant is started? *Why?*

19. When a gasoline engine is being checked for free turning prior to starting, why should the starting switch not be held in the START position for more than 30 seconds?

20. If a gasoline engine fails to start with the aid of the primer in extremely cold weather, which additional measure may be taken to facilitate starting?

21. When a gasoline engine equipped with a battery- and booster-coil starting system is being started, which parts, in addition to the starting motor, may be damaged if the starter switch is held in the START position for more than 30 seconds?

22. Give the *advantages* of completing the warm-up of the gasoline-engine power-plant of a boat after the boat is under way.

KEY (CORRECT ANSWERS)

1. The lubricating oil pump(s) must be in operation.

2. One type of device is used to heat the intake air or a portion of the cylinder charge; another type is used to supply an auxiliary, low-ignition-temperature fuel to the cylinders during the starting period.

3. Electric, and fuel oil.

4. Ether.

5. Because of uneven rates of expansion of engine parts and inadequate lubrication.

6. The lubricating oil may be diluted; fuel consumption may be increased.

7. Excessive temperatures, excessive pressures, and smoky exhaust.

8. (1) Mechanical oilers, if provided, should be checked frequently for proper feed;
   (2) the oil level in the sump should be checked frequently and oil should be added, as necessary;
   (3) purifiers, if provided, should be operated in accordance with prescribed instructions;
   (4) cleaning handles of all oil strainers should be rotated at recommended intervals; and
   (5) the viscosity of the oil should be checked at least once each day.

9. (1) Salt-water cooling system;
   (2) fresh-water cooling system;
   (3) lubricating-oil system.

4

10. By regulating the amount of water discharged, by the pump, into the engine; by regulating the amount of water which passes through the cooler.

11. In the fresh-water discharge line from the engine.

12. To any range of engine speed during which excessive vibration is created in the engine.

13. So that the operating condition of the device can be checked.

14. When provided, independent water-pumps and lubricating-oil pumps are operated for a short period of time.

15. The engine should be stopped, and the cause of the popping should be determined and remedied.

16. Steps must be taken to ensure that there is no gasoline vapor in the engineroom or in other spaces. These steps will vary, depending on the installation; they may include, however, such items as operating the engineroom exhaust-blower and opening the engine head, or casing, to permit free circulation of air.

17. So that the oil level in the crankcase can be checked when the engine is not operating and when the boat is under way.

18. The tank with the highest level should be used, so that the tanks can be kept as nearly balanced as possible.

19. So that the starting motor will not be overheated and damaged.

20. The carburetor and the intake manifold may be heated by wrapping them in rags and then applying boiling water to the rags.

21. The coil, which may overheat; and the points, which may burn.

22. Less time is required for completing the warm-up; the tendency of the spark plugs to foul is reduced.

————

TEST 3

DIRECTIONS: Answer the following questions directly, briefly, and succinctly.

QUESTIONS

1. What is meant by progressive maintenance?

2. For most efficient operation, should the handle of a metal-edge strainer be turned
    (a) when fluid is passing through the strainer; or
    (b) when the strainer is not in use?

3. When a metal-edge strainer is being prepared for disassembly and cleaning, why should the oil drained from the strainer case be caught in a clean container and be retained?

4. For which type of trouble should a screen-type strainer be checked, after it has been cleaned?

5. Under which conditions may the element of a filter be washed?

6. To what extent may a zinc be allowed to deteriorate before replacement is made?

7. Give *two* methods by which heat exchangers may be cleaned and indicate the types of heat exchangers which may be cleaned by each method.

8. Give *three* reasons why the sea-water side of the element in an oil cooler may become clogged.

9. Name *four* approved tools which may be used in cleaning the element of a shell-and-tube cooler.

10. What are the *two* chemicals used to treat the water in the closed, cooling-water circuit of an internal combustion engine?

11. Why is it *desirable* to maintain the fresh water in the closed circuit of an engine cooling system in a slightly alkaline condition?

12. Name the *three* tests which are used to determine the condition of treated, engine-cooling water.

13. What is indicated when an alkalinity test of cooling water causes the test sample to turn yellow?

14. What trouble will occur if the sodium-chromate concentration in treated, engine-cooling water drops below 900 ppm? *Why?*

15. To which of the concentrations in treated cooling water do the following limits apply?
    (a) Between 900 and 1100 ppm;
    (b) below 100 ppm;
    (c) pH 8-10.

KEY (CORRECT ANSWERS)

1. The inspection and repair of the major engine components, one at a time, until the entire engine has been progressively inspected and overhauled during the recommended period of time between major overhauls.

2. (b) When the strainer is not in use.

3. So that the oil may be checked for metal particles which are an indication of trouble inside the engine.

4. Ruptures.

5. Olly in emergencies, when new elements are not available and the engine must be operated.

6. Zincs which are more than one-half deteriorated should be replaced.

7. Mechanical cleaning, used in cleaning shell-and-tube coolers; chemical cleaning, used in cleaning coolers of the radiator and plate types.

8. Faulty operation of the strainer; improper lubrication of the water pump; and a leaking element.

9. Air lance, water lance, bristle brush (rotating), and rubber plugs.

10. Boiler compound and sodium dichromate.

11. Slight alkalinity counteracts acid corrosion.

12. Alkalinity, sodium chromate, and chloride tests.

13. The water-treatment solution contains insufficient boiler compound.

14. The parts within the cooling system may corrode.

15. (a) Sodium chromate; (b) chloride; (c) alkalinity.

TEST 4

DIRECTIONS: Answer the following questions directly, briefly, and succinctly.

QUESTIONS

1. In most large, modern engines, which type of pump is used to circulate the water in the engine cooling system?

2. Why are positive-displacement pumps fitted with bypass valves?

3. Name *two* types of reciprocating pumps that are used in engine installations.

4. What is the *most common* cause of the failure of a sea-water circulating pump to take suction?

5. Give *three* symptoms which indicate that the shaft of a centrifugal water-pump may have broken.

6. When the stuffing box of a water pump is being repacked, should the joints of succeeding packing rings be lined up evenly, or should they be staggered?

7. Why is it necessary to allow a slight amount of leakage between a pump shaft and its packing?

8. What is likely to happen if a centrifugal pump is operated dry?

9. What should be done in order to determine visually if the seat and the disk of a globe valve are making satisfactory contact?

10. After a globe valve has been ground-in, how should you check the contact surfaces of the seat and the disk?

11. How can overgrinding of a valve seat or disk be corrected?

12. Under which circumstances is the lapping process used to re-finish the seating surfaces of a globe valve?

13. What should be done to the seating surfaces of a globe valve after the lapping process has been completed?

14. How many grades of compound are needed to complete the lapping of a valve in which the seat is damaged extensively?

15. Give the steps which may be necessary if leakage occurs at the stuffing box of a globe valve in which the valve stem is in good condition.

16. When the stuffing box of a valve is being repacked with string-type packing, why should the packing be wound in the same direction as the gland nut is turned for tightening?

17. When a plug-cock valve in a cooling system is being lubricated, what precaution must be taken to prevent the lubricant from being forced into the water stream?

KEY (CORRECT ANSWERS)

1. Centrifugal.

2. So that the pumped liquid may be recirculated to the suction side of the pump, when the amount of liquid being pumped is greater than the amount required.

3. (a) Plunger-type pumps; and
   (b) diaphragm-type pumps.

4. A clogged strainer.

5. (a) Noise of breakage;
   (b) a rise in cooling-water temperature; and
   (c) loss of discharge pressure.

6. They should be staggered.

7. To provide lubrication for the packing, and to carry heat away from the packing gland.

8. Heat generated by friction within the pump may expand the impeller so much that it will seize the casing.

9. The seat and the disk should be spotted-in.

10. By spotting-in the disk to the seat.

11. Only by machining.

12. Only when the valve seat contains irregularities that cannot be satisfactorily removed by grinding-in.

13. A disk should be spotted-in and ground-in to the seat.

14. Four.

15. Set up on the gland; if this fails to stop the leakage, repack the stuffing box.

16. To prevent the packing from folding back when the gland is tightened.

17. Make sure that the valve is either wide open or fully closed.

—————

TEST 5

QUESTIONS

1. What is meant by compressor displacement?

2. Vessels which require only a small supply of high-pressure air are equipped with compressors having how many stages?

3. What causes automatic action of the air valves on modern air compressors?

4. What keeps compressed air from forcing the oil back into the cylinder lubricator of an air compressor?

5. How is the oil which lubricates the running gear of an air compressor returned to the reservoir?

6. On late model water-cooled air compressors, what provision is made to regulate temperature in the oil cooler without affecting the temperature in other parts of the cooling system?

7. What function is performed by the intercoolers of an air compressor?

8. Why are the intercoolers and aftercoolers of an air compressor fitted with separators?

9. When the automatic shutdown device stops the compressor, will the compressor restart automatically?

10. Which type of control is installed when a compressor is required to furnish a continuous supply of air?

11. Is the compressor control device that is used to ensure a continuous supply of air actuated by changes in
    (a) temperature, or
    (b) pressure?

12. What can be accomplished with dual control on an air compressor?

13. Describe briefly the path of air through a *three-stage* compressor, by listing, in the proper sequence, the parts through which the air flows.

14. Why should benzine, kerosene, and similar oils *NEVER* be used to clean the filters, cylinders, or air passages of an air compressor?

15. From which *three* general causes may explosions occur within an air-compressor element, the discharge line, or the air receiver?

16. When the temperature of the air discharged from any stage of compression exceeds the maximum operating temperature, should
    (a) the amount of cooling water be increased,
    (b) the setting of the relief valve on the water side of the intercooler be adjusted, or
    (c) the compressor be secured?

17. When work is being performed on the compressor, should the valves between the air compressor and the receiver be opened or closed?

18. What is the *most probable* cause of trouble when a P-500 pump fails to take suction as the pump is started?

19. How is lubricating oil supplied to the engine parts on a P-500 pump?

20. What is indicated when the hand primer of a P-500 pump suddenly becomes hard to pump?

21. Give *two* symptoms which indicate that the fuel supply of a P-500 pump is nearly exhausted.

———

KEY (CORRECT ANSWERS)

1. The volume of air displaced by first-stage piston(s) on compression strokes.

2. Three.

3. The difference in pressure between the air within the cylinder and the air on the external surfaces of the intake and discharge valves.

4. A check valve installed at the end of each cylinder feed-line.

5. By gravity.

6. Valves are arranged so that the quantity of cooling water passing through the oil cooler may be regulated without changing the quantity of water circulating through the rest of the system.

7. They cool the compressed air, between stages of compression.

8. To remove water and oil from the compressed air.

9. No.

10. Constant-speed control.

11. Pressure.

12. The operator can set the controls so that the compressor will operate under either start-stop control or constant-speed control.

13. Air-intake filter; first-stage compressing element(s); first-stage intercooler; second-stage compressing element; second-stage intercooler; third-stage compressing element; aftercooler; and air receiver.

14. Fumes may collect and cause an explosion in the compressor or in the receiver.

15. (1) Dust-laden intake air;
    (2) oil vapor in the compressor or in the receiver; and
    (3) abnormally high temperature resulting from leaky or dirty air-valves.

16. The compressor should be secured.

17. The valves should be closed.

18. Air leakage, through a poor connection, into the suction side.

19. The lubricating oil is mixed with the engine fuel.

20. That air has been exhausted from the pump and that water has entered the pump.

21. Irregular engine operation; lowered position of the float-pin in the carburetor bowl.

BASIC FUNDAMENTALS OF ENGINES, FUELS, LUBRICANTS, AND POLLUTION CONTROL

As an equipment operator, you will be mainly concerned with operation of equipment. In order to perform these duties intelligently, it is important that you fully understand the principles of the internal combustion engine operation and the function of the various components that make up the internal combustion engine. This understanding will make your job easier when simple adjustments or repairs have to be made.

This chapter discusses basic principles of engine operation and explains some of the terminology related to engines. Various types of fuel and lubricants are described and information is given on the safe handling and storage of petroleum products. Information is provided on the types and purposes of filters used on automotive and construction equipment. Various methods are discussed on environmental pollution control so that you may effectively control pollution resulting from the combustion and spillage of fuels.

I. INTERNAL COMBUSTION ENGINES

An internal combustion engine is one in which the fuel burns within the body of the engine. The burning that takes place inside the cylinders produces the energy that turns the crankshaft of the engine. Both gasoline and diesel engines operate on this principle.

Combustion is the act or process of burning. An internal or external combustion engine is defined simply as a machine that converts this heat energy to mechanical energy. To fulfill this purpose, the engine may take one of several forms.

With the internal combustion engine, combustion takes place inside the cylinder and is directly responsible for forcing the piston to move down.

In external combustion engines, such as steam engines, combustion takes place outside the engine. Figure 1 shows, in simplified form, an external and an internal combustion engine.

The external combustion engine requires a boiler to which heat is applied. This combustion causes water to boil to produce steam. The steam passes into the engine cylinder under pressure and forces the piston to move downward.

The transformation of HEAT ENERGY to MECHANICAL ENERGY by the engine is based on a fundamental law of physics which states that gas will expand upon application of heat. If the gas is confined with no outlet for expansion, then the pressure of the gas will be increased when heat is applied. In the internal combustion engine the burning of a fuel within a closed cylinder results in an expansion of gases, thus creating a pressure on top of a piston and causing it to move downward.

In an internal combustion engine the piston moves up and down within a cylinder. This up-and-down motion is known as RECIPROCATING MOTION. This reciprocating motion (straight line motion) must be changed to ROTARY MOTION (turning motion) in order to turn the wheels of a vehicle. A crankshaft and a connecting rod change this reciprocating motion to rotary motion, figure 2.

All internal combustion engines, whether gasoline or diesel, are basically the same. We can best demonstrate this by saying they all rely on three things — AIR, FUEL, and IGNITION.

FUEL contains potential energy for operating the engine; AIR contains the oxygen necessary for combustion; and IGNITION starts combustion. All are fundamental, and the engine will not operate without any one of them. Any discussion of engines must be based on these three factors and the steps and mechanisms involved in delivering them to the combustion chamber at the proper time.

The power of an internal combustion engine comes from the burning of a mixture of fuel and air in a small, enclosed space. When this

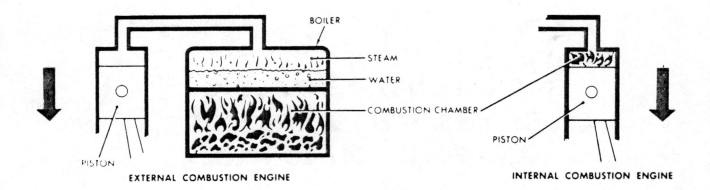

Figure 1. — Simple external and internal combustion engine.

mixture burns it expands greatly, and the push or pressure created is used to move the piston, thereby rotating the crankshaft. This movement is eventually sent back to the wheels to drive the vehicle.

Since similar action occurs in all cylinders of an engine, let's use one cylinder in our development of power. The one-cylinder engine consists of four basic parts as shown in figure 2.

First we must have a CYLINDER which is closed at one end; this cylinder is similar to a tall metal can which is stationary within the engine block. Inside this cylinder is the PISTON,

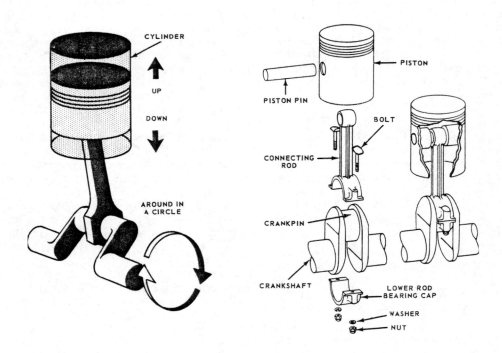

Figure 2. — Cylinder, piston, connecting rod, and crankshaft for one-cylinder engine.

a movable metal plug, which fits snugly into the cylinder, but can still slide up and down easily.

You have already learned that the up-and-down movement of the piston is called reciprocating motion. This motion must be changed to rotary motion so the wheels or tracks of vehicles can be made to rotate. This change is accomplished by a crank on the CRANKSHAFT and a CONNECTING ROD which connects the piston and the crank.

The crank is an offset section of the crankshaft, which scribes a circle as the shaft rotates. The top end of the connecting rod is connected to the piston and must, therefore, go up and down. The lower end of the connecting rod also moves up and down but, because it is attached to the crankshaft, it must also move in a circle with the crank.

When the piston of the engine slides downward because of the pressure of the expanding gases in the cylinder, the upper end of the connecting rod moves downward with the piston, in a straight line. The lower end of the connecting rod moves down and in a circular motion at the same time. This moves the crank which, in turn, rotates the shaft; this rotation is the desired result. So remember, the crankshaft and connecting rod combination is a mechanism for the purpose of changing straight line (or reciprocating) motion to circular (or rotary) motion.

FOUR-STROKE CYCLE
GASOLINE ENGINE

The operating principles of the gasoline and diesel engines are basically the same. Therefore, only the operating cycles of the four-stroke gasoline engine and the two-stroke cycle diesel engines will be discussed.

Each movement of the piston from top to bottom or from bottom to top is called a stroke. The piston takes two strokes (an upstroke and a downstroke) as the crankshaft makes one complete revolution. When the piston is at the top of a stroke (fig. 3), it is said to be at top dead center (TDC). When the piston is at the bottom of a stroke (fig. 4), it is said to be at bottom dead center (BDC).

The basic engine you have studied so far has no provisions for getting the fuel-air mixture into the cylinder or burned gases out of the cylinder. There are two openings in the closed end of a cylinder. One of the openings, permits an intake of air or an intake of a mixture of fuel and air into the combustion area of the cylinder. The other opening permits the burned

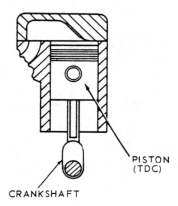

Figure 3. — Piston top dead center (TDC).

gases to escape from the cylinder. The two openings have valves in them. These valves, activated by the camshaft, close off either one or the other of the openings, or both of them during various stages of engine operation. The camshaft has a number of cams along its length that open the valves and hold them open for the correct length of time during the piston stroke. The camshaft is driven by the crankshaft through timing gears, or by means of a timing chain. On a 4-stroke cycle engine (fig. 5) the camshaft turns at one-half crankshaft speed. This permits each valve to open and close once for every two revolutions of the crankshaft. One of the valves, called the intake valve, opens to admit an intake of air or a mixture of fuel

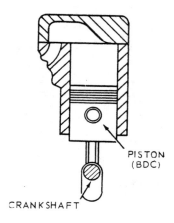

Figure 4. — Piston bottom dead center (BDC).

3

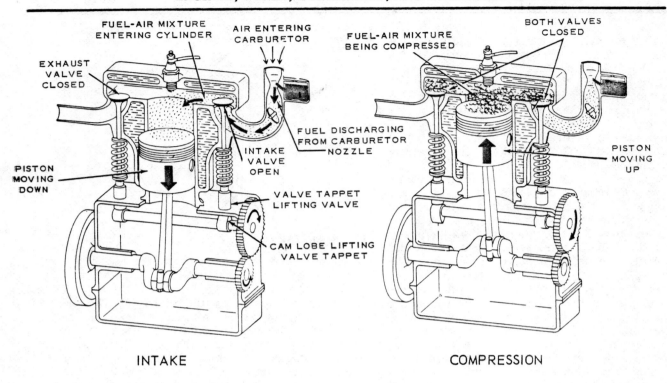

INTAKE

COMPRESSION

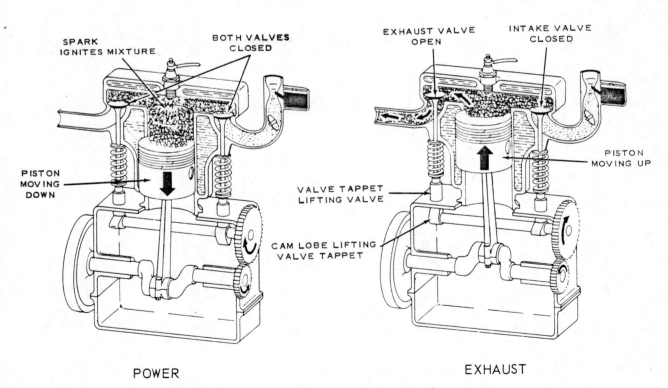

POWER

EXHAUST

Figure 5. — Four-stroke cycle in a gasoline engine.

and air into the cylinder. The other valve, called the exhaust valve, opens to allow the escape of burned gases after the fuel-and-air mixture has burned.

The following paragraphs give a simplified explanation of the action that takes place within the engine cylinder.

Intake Stroke

The first stroke in the sequence is called the INTAKE stroke (fig. 5). During this stroke, as the crankshaft continues to rotate, the piston is moving downward and the intake valve is open. This downward movement of the piston produces a partial vacuum in the cylinder, and an air-fuel mixture rushes into the cylinder past the open intake valve. This is somewhat the same effect as when you drink through a straw. A partial vacuum is produced in the mouth and the liquid moves up through the straw to fill the vacuum.

Compression Stroke

When the piston reaches bottom dead center at the end of the intake stroke and is therefore at the bottom of the cylinder, the intake valve closes. This seals the upper end of the cylinder. As the crankshaft continues to rotate, it pushes up, through the connecting rod, on the piston. The piston is therefore pushed upward and compresses the combustible mixture in the cylinder; this is called the COMPRESSION stroke (fig. 5). In gasoline engines, the mixture is compressed to about one-eighth of its original volume, which is called an 8 to 1 compression ratio. This compression of the air-fuel mixture increases the pressure within the cylinder. Compressing the mixture in this way makes it still more combustible; not only does the pressure in the cylinder go up, but the temperature of the mixture also increases.

Power Stroke

As the piston reaches top dead center at the end of the compression stroke and therefore has moved to the top of the cylinder, the compressed fuel-air mixture is ignited. The ignition system causes an electric spark to occur suddenly in the cylinder, and the spark ignites the compressed fuel-air mixture. In burning, the mixture gets very hot and tries to expand in all directions. The pressure rises to about 600 to 700 pounds per square inch. Since the

piston is the only thing that can move, the force produced by the expanding gases forces the piston down. This force, or thrust, is carried through the connecting rod to the crankpin on the crankshaft. The crankshaft is given a powerful turn. This is called the POWER stroke (fig. 5). This turning effort, rapidly repeated in the engine and carried through gears and shafts, will turn the wheels of a vehicle and cause it to move along the highway.

Exhaust Stroke

After the fuel-air mixture has burned, it must be cleared from the cylinder. This is done by opening the exhaust valve just as the power stroke is finished and the piston starts back up on the EXHAUST stroke (fig. 5). The piston forces the burned gases out of the cylinder past the open exhaust valve.

ENGINE CYCLES

The four strokes (intake, compression, power, and exhaust) are continuously repeated as the engine runs. Now, with the basic knowledge you have of the parts and the four strokes of the engine, let us see what happens during the actual running of the engine. To produce sustained power, an engine must accomplish the same series of events — intake, compression, power, and exhaust — over and over again.

This series of events is called a cycle. Remember that in a 4-stroke cycle engine it takes four complete strokes of the piston to complete one engine cycle, that is, two complete revolutions of the crankshaft. Most engines that you will deal with are of the 4-stroke cycle design.

2-Stroke Cycle Diesel Engine

In the 2-stroke cycle engine, the same four events (intake, compression, power, and exhaust) take place in only two strokes of the piston; one complete revolution of the crankshaft.

The 2-stroke cycle operation shown in figure 6 features the General Motors 71 series. This engine differs in two ways from the 4-stroke cycle engine previously discussed. Not only does it complete the four events in 2-strokes, but it depends upon the heat of compression rather than a spark for ignition. In the two-cycle engine, intake and exhaust take place during part of the compression and power strokes respectively.

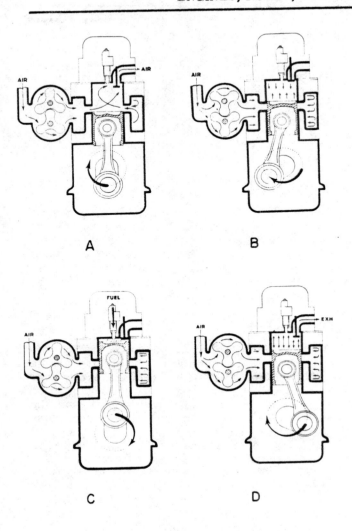

Figure 6.— Events in a 2-stroke cycle, internal combustion engine.

In contrast, a four-cycle engine requires four piston strokes to complete an operating cycle. A blower is provided to force air into the cylinders for expelling the exhaust gases and supply the cylinders with fresh air for combustion. The cylinder walls contain a row of ports which are above the piston when it is at the bottom of its stroke. These ports admit the air from the blower into the cylinder as soon as the top face of the piston uncovers the ports, as shown in view A, figure 6. The indirectional flow of air toward the exhaust valves produces a scavenging effect; this action leaves the cylinder full of clean air when the piston again covers the inlet ports.

As the piston continues on the upward stroke, the exhaust valves (2 per cylinder) close and the charge of fresh air is subject to compression, as shown in view B, figure 6. Shortly before the piston reaches its highest position, the required amount of fuel is sprayed into the combustion space by the cylinder's injector, view C, figure 6; the intense heat generated during the high compression of the air ignites the fine spray immediately and the combustion continues as long as the fuel spray lasts. The resulting pressure forces the piston downward on the power stroke. The exhaust valves are again opened when the piston is about halfway down, allowing the combustion gases to escape into the exhaust manifold, view D, figure 6. Shortly thereafter, the downward movement of the piston uncovers the inlet ports and the cylinder is again swept with clean air, as shown in view A, figure 6. This entire combustion cycle is completed in each cylinder for each revolution of the crankshaft and during two strokes of the piston thus; the term "two-stroke cycle."

4-Stroke Cycle Vs
2-Stroke Cycle

A power stroke is produced every crankshaft revolution within the 2-stroke cycle engine; whereas the 4-stroke cycle engine requires two crankshaft revolutions for one power stroke.

It might appear then that a 2-stroke cycle could produce twice as much power as a 4-stroke cycle of the same size, operating at the same speed. However, this is not true. With some 2-stroke cycle engines, some of the power is used to drive a blower that forces the air-fuel charge into the cylinder under pressure. Also, the burned gases are not completely cleared from the cylinder, reducing combustion efficiency. Additionally, because of the much shorter period the intake port is open (as compared to the period the intake valve in a 4-stroke-cycle is open), a relatively smaller amount of fuel-air mixture is admitted. Hence, with less fuel-air mixture, less power per power stroke is produced in a 2-stroke cycle engine of like size operating at the same speed and with other conditions being the same.

MULTIFUEL ENGINE

The multifuel engine operates on a compression ignition, four-stroke cycle principle similar to conventional four-stroke cycle diesel and gasoline engines. Those pieces of military equipment which are equipped with the multifuel engine are designed to use several different types of fuel, such as gasoline, kerosene, diesel, and (JP) fuels. No modifications or adjustments are necessary when changing grades or types of fuel.

The multifuel engine operation cycle, is shown in figure 7.

STARTING AND STOPPING PROCEDURES
FOR GASOLINE AND DIESEL ENGINES

In the previous sections you learned about the operating cycle of the internal combustion engine, and how it is constructed.

In order to make the basic engine operational, it requires the addition of cooling, lubrication, fuel, and electrical systems. Before starting an internal combustion engine, certain pre-start checks must be made to determine if the engine will operate. Check for fuel, coolant, battery condition, loose wires, oil level, and the absence of leaks.

In this chapter, it is infeasible to state the correct procedures for starting and stopping every type of automotive or construction equipment, equipped with a gasoline or diesel engine that is used. Therefore, the procedures explained below apply to typical types of automotive equipment equipped with a gasoline engine. For information on a specific type of automotive vehicle consult the manufacturers operating manual. Procedures for starting and stopping a typical piece of construction equipment equipped with a diesel engine are covered in chapter 9.

Before starting the engine, be sure the hand or parking brake is set, and the gear selector lever is in NEUTRAL. On a vehicle with an automatic transmission, set the lever at N (NEUTRAL) or push in the N (NEUTRAL) button; otherwise the engine will not start. Some vehicles can be started also in P (PARK).

Next, turn on the ignition and depress the accelerator one-quarter of the way toward the floor. If the equipment has a clutch, disengage it before starting the engine to ensure that the vehicle will not move, and to keep the starter from turning the transmission.

If the engine does not have an automatic choke, pull the choke control out about half-way. Using the choke when the engine is warm will cause flooding and will hinder easy starting.

Now operate the starter until the engine begins to fire. The starter on some vehicles may be actuated by pushing in a starter button on the instrument panel; on others, by depressing the starter button on the floorboard. A few engines are started by depressing the accelerator pedal; on others, turning the ignition switch key to the extreme right starts the engine.

If the engine does not start within 10 seconds, stop to see whether you have properly performed all prestarting operations. If it does not start after several attempts, notify your chief.

Caution: Never operate the cranking motor for more than 30 seconds at a time. If the engine fails to start in 30 seconds, allow the cranking motor to cool for 2 to 3 minutes before resuming cranking operation. Prolonged use of the starter wears it out and discharges the battery.

As soon as the engine begins to fire, release the starter knob, or let the ignition switch key snap back to ON position. Release the clutch pedal slowly, if you have depressed it, and push the choke control back in. After the engine is operating smoothly, ease off the throttle, and allow the engine to idle till it warms to the proper operating temperature. The warm-up period allows the oil in the crankcase to circulate and lubricate the engine pistons, bearings, and the cylinder surfaces. Putting a vehicle into motion before the engine is at proper operating temperature will cause undue wear of the moving parts of the engine.

The following are typical procedures for stopping automotive gasoline engines: (1) Allow the engine to operate at low idle for 3 to 5 minutes, (2) check gage readings; for water coolant within normal range, lubricating oil pressure within range, ammeter showing a charge, fuel gage indicating sufficient fule, and air pressure gage (if so equipped) indicating normal air pressure, and (3) turn the electrical system ignition switch to the OFF position.

II. FUELS AND LUBRICANTS

Fuels and lubricants for gasoline and diesel engines are byproducts of petroleum. Petroleum, often called crude oil, means "rock oil." Petroleum products include gasoline, kerosene, diesel fuel, lubricating oils, gear lubricants, and greases. Many different products are added to the raw byproducts to obtain a fuel or lubricant that will perform efficiently in modern equipment.

Crude oil would ruin an engine if the impurities were not removed. The impurities are removed by the refining process, which also

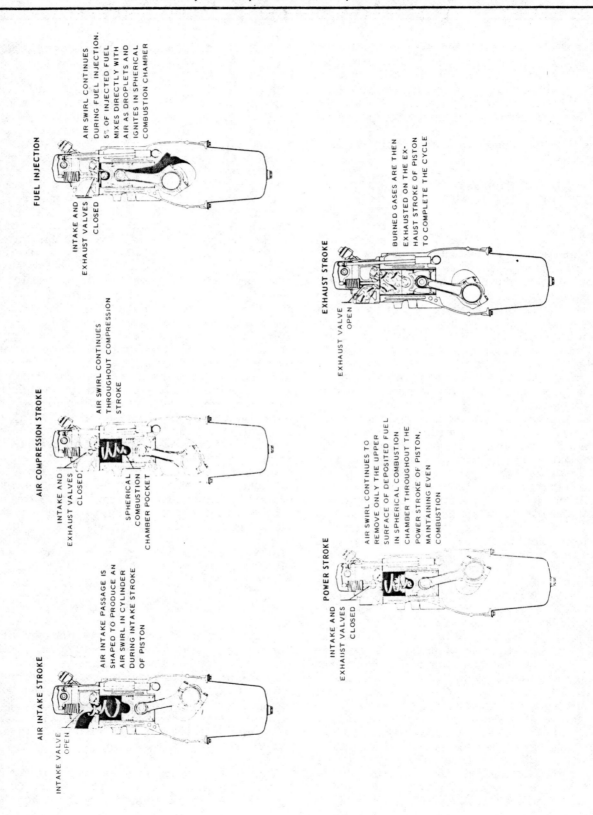

AIR INTAKE STROKE

INTAKE VALVE OPEN

AIR INTAKE PASSAGE IS SHAPED TO PRODUCE AN AIR SWIRL IN CYLINDER DURING INTAKE STROKE OF PISTON

AIR COMPRESSION STROKE

INTAKE AND EXHAUST VALVES CLOSED

AIR SWIRL CONTINUES THROUGHOUT COMPRESSION STROKE

SPHERICAL COMBUSTION CHAMBER POCKET

FUEL INJECTION

INTAKE AND EXHAUST VALVES CLOSED

AIR SWIRL CONTINUES DURING FUEL INJECTION. 5% OF INJECTED FUEL MIXES DIRECTLY WITH AIR AS DROPLETS AND IGNITES IN SPHERICAL COMBUSTION CHAMBER

POWER STROKE

INTAKE AND EXHAUST VALVES CLOSED

AIR SWIRL CONTINUES TO REMOVE ONLY THE UPPER SURFACE OF DEPOSITED FUEL IN SPHERICAL COMBUSTION CHAMBER THROUGHOUT THE POWER STROKE OF PISTON, MAINTAINING EVEN COMBUSTION

EXHAUST STROKE

EXHAUST VALVE OPEN

BURNED GASES ARE THEN EXHAUSTED ON THE EXHAUST STROKE OF PISTON TO COMPLETE THE CYCLE

Figure · 7. — Multifuel engine operation cycles.

separates the oil into various petroleum products. (See fig. 8.)

You have seen a teakettle boil. Heating the water in the kettle changes it to gas or vapor in the form of steam at a certain temperature. Many kinds of liquids change to gases, or are said to VAPORIZE, at different temperatures. Heating petroleum, which is a mixture of liquids, will change the liquids to gases one by one. Cooling changes each gas back to liquid form through condensation. This process of separating substances from one another is called DISTILLATION.

Distillation drives gasoline vapors from the crude oil first, because gasoline has a lower boiling point and vaporizes before other petroleum products. Substances with higher boiling points, like kerosene and the gas-oil from which we get most of our diesel fuel, are given off next. After the gas-oil has been collected, lubricating oils are distilled, the lightest first (lube distillates), and then the heavier ones (commonly called bottoms). (It is to be noted, bottoms are where we get asphaltic products.) (See fig. 8.)

You will hear also about propane and butane fuels, which are byproducts of natural gas. (Notice in figure 3-8 that gas is taken from a cavity in the earth that is between the oil and the rock formation just above the oil.) These liquids must be collected and stored under pressure because they change into gas when released to the atmosphere. Liquid propane becomes a gas at a temperature of -43°F; liquid butane, at -33°F. Although seldom used as a fuel for automotive equipment, small amounts of these liquid gases have been used to start engines in very cold climates. Some manufacturers believe that internal combustion engines can operate more economically with butane fuel than with gasoline. Gasoline and diesel oil, however, continue to be the most common fuels for internal combustion engines.

PROPERTIES OF GASOLINE

Gasoline contains carbon and hydrogen in such proportions that the gasoline burns freely and liberates HEAT ENERGY. If all the potential heat energy contained in a gallon of gasoline could be converted into work, a motor vehicle could run hundreds of miles on each gallon. However, only a small percentage of this heat energy is converted into power by the engine. Most authorities consider the power losses within the engine to be as follows:

Engine	Percent of Power Loss
Cooling System	35
Exhaust Gases	35
Engine Friction	5 to 10
Total	75 to 80

The question of what is ideal gasoline is more theoretical than practical. Every manufacturer recommends the octane rating of the gasoline he feels is best for the engines he produces. Besides engine design, factors like the weight of the vehicle, the terrain and highways over which it is to be driven, and the climate and altitude of the locality also determine what gasoline is best to use. All other factors being equal, these may be considered as some of the properties of the best gasoline: good antiknock quality, a minimum content of foreign matter, and a volatility which makes starting easy and allows smooth acceleration and economical operation.

Volatility

The blend of a gasoline determines its VOLATILITY—that is, its tendency to change from a liquid to a vapor at any given temperature. The rate of vaporization increases as the temperature of the gasoline rises.

No standard for gasoline volatility meets all engine operating requirements. The volatility must be high enough for easy starting and acceleration. Ordinarily the proper starting mixture is about 15 parts of air to 1 part of fuel, but in very cold weather more fuel must be admitted to the cylinders through the use of the choke in the carburetor for quicker starting. In polar regions, a gasoline of higher volatility makes starting easier; it also helps keep the crankcase from becoming diluted by gasoline seeping past the piston and the piston rings while the engine is being choked.

On the other hand, a gasoline of low volatility brings about better fuel economy and combats VAPOR LOCK (the formation of vapor in the fuel lines in a quantity sufficient to block the flow of gasoline through the system). In the summer and in hot climates, especially, fuels with low volatility lessen the tendency toward vapor lock.

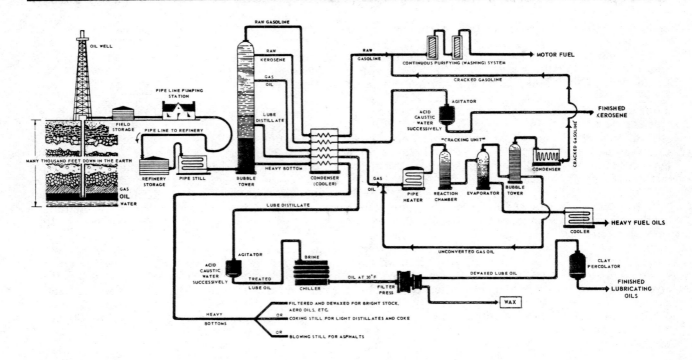

Figure 8. — Typical chart tracing crude oil from well to finished product.

Purity

Engine efficiency depends to some extent on the PURITY of gasoline. Gums and sulfur are removed from crude oil in the refining process. Gums in gasoline cause sticking valves and form hard baked surfaces within the cylinders. Residue unites with moisture to form sulfuric acid, which corrodes engine parts. Modern refining processes have reduced the sulfur and other foreign matter content of gasoline, thus minimizing the damage to engine parts as well as cutting down engine maintenance.

Antiknock Quality and
Detonation

Reviewing the process of combustion will help you understand the ANTIKNOCK quality of gasoline. When any substance burns, its molecules and those of the oxygen in the air around it are set into motion, producing heat that unites the two groups of molecules in a rapid chemical reaction. In the combustion chamber of an engine cylinder, the gasoline vapor and oxygen in the air are ignited and burn. They combine, and the molecules begin to move about very rapidly, as the high temperatures of combustion are reached. This rapid movement of molecules provides the push on the piston to force it downward on the power stroke.

In the modern high compression gasoline engines the air-fuel mixture tends to ignite spontaneously or to explode instead of burning. The result is a knock, a ping, or a DETONATION. In detonation the spark from the spark plug starts the fuel mixture burning, and the flame spreads through the layers of the mixture, very quickly compressing and heating them. The last layers become so compressed and heated that they explode violently. The explosive pressure strikes the piston head and the walls of the cylinder, and causes the knock you hear in the engine. It is the fuel, not the engine, that knocks. Besides being an annoying sound, persistent knocking results in engine overheating, loss of power, and increased fuel consumption. It causes severe shock to the spark plugs, pistons, connecting rods, and the crankshaft. To slow down this burning rate of the fuel, a fuel of a higher octane rating must be used.

10

Octane Rating

The property of a fuel to resist detonation is called its antiknock or OCTANE rating. The octane rating is obtained by comparing the antiknock qualities of gasoline in a special test engine against reference fuels.

Octane numbers range from 50 in cheaper gasolines to over 100 for those required of modern high compression engines. The octane number has nothing to do with the starting qualities, potential energy, or volatility of the fuel.

The octane rating of gasoline can be raised in two ways: by mixing it with another fuel, or treating it with a chemical. In this country a chemical is added to gasoline to improve its octane rating. The most efficient additive used for this purpose is tetraethyl lead compound, which is added to the gasoline with ETHYL FLUID. In addition to the tetraethyl lead, ethyl fluid contains other chemicals that prevent lead deposits from forming within the engine. Lead oxide causes considerable corrosion.

The LEAD CONTENT of ethyl fluid is very poisonous. Ethyl gasoline should be used only for engine fuel and for no other purpose. It should never be used as a cleaning agent.

An engine which does not knock on a low octane fuel will not operate more efficiently by using a fuel of high octane rating. An engine which knocks on a given fuel should use one of a higher rating. If a higher octane fuel does not stop the knocking, some mechanical adjustments are probably necessary. Retarding the spark so that the engine will fire later may end knocking. However, an engine operating on retarded spark will use more fuel and will overheat. It may be less expensive to use a higher priced, high-octane gasoline with an advanced spark than to use a cheap, low-octane gasoline with a retarded spark.

Engine knocking is not always the result of using too low an octane rating; it can be caused by preignition. In preignition the fuel-air mixture begins to burn before the spark occurs. This condition may be caused by an overheated exhaust valve head, hot spark plugs, or glowing pieces of carbon within the combustion chamber. In figure 9, you see the diagrammed course of the fuel-air mixture in the cylinder under circumstances of preignition and detonation, as well as in normal combustion.

DIESEL FUEL

Diesel fuel is heavier than gasoline because it is obtained from the residue of the crude oil after the more volatile fuels have been removed. As with gasoline, the efficiency of a diesel fuel varies with the type of engine in which it is used. By distillation, cracking, and blending of several oils, a suitable diesel fuel can be obtained for almost all engine operating conditions. Slow speed diesels use a wide variety of heavy fuels; high speed diesel engines require a lighter fuel. Using a poor or an improper grade of fuel can cause hard starting, incomplete combustion, a smoky exhaust, and engine knocks.

The properties to be considered in selecting a fuel for a diesel engine are VOLATILITY, CLEANLINESS, VISCOSITY, AND IGNITION QUALITY.

Volatility

The volatility of a diesel fuel is measured by the 90 percent distillation temperature. This is the temperature at which 90 percent of a sample of the fuel has been distilled off. The lower this temperature, the higher the volatility of the fuel. In small diesel engines, a fuel of high volatility is more necessary than in large engines if there is to be low fuel consumption, low exhaust temperature, and little exhaust smoke.

Cleanliness

Cleanliness of diesel fuel is very important. Fuel should not contain more than a trace of foreign substances; otherwise, fuel pump and injector difficulties will develop. Because it is heavier and more viscous, diesel fuel will hold dirt particles in suspension for longer periods than will gasoline. In the refining process, not all foreign matter can be removed, and harmful matter like dirt and water can get into the fuel while it is being handled. Water will cause hard starting and misfiring. Dirt will clog injectors and spray nozzles and may cause an engine to misfire or stop altogether.

Viscosity

The viscosity of fuel is the measure of its resistance to flow. Viscosity is expressed by the number of seconds required for a certain volume of fuel to flow through a hole of a certain diameter at a given temperature. The viscosity of diesel duel must be low enough to flow

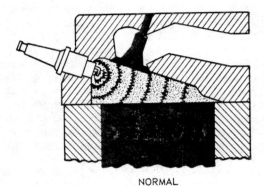

NORMAL

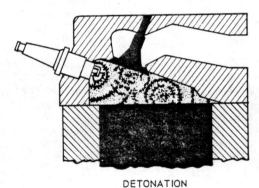

DETONATION

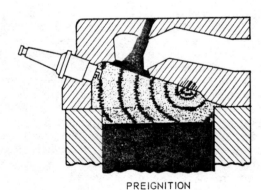

PREIGNITION

Figure 9. — Combustion process.

freely at low temperatures, yet high enough to lubricate the pump and injector plungers properly and lessen the possibility of leakage at the pump plungers and dribbling at the injectors. Viscosity is measured by an instrument (fig. 10) called the SAYBOLT VISCOSIMETER and is expressed in SAYBOLT SECONDS, UNIVERSAL (SSU).

A Saybolt viscosimeter consists of an oil tube, a constant-temperature oil bath which maintains the correct temperature of the sample in the tube, a 60-cc (cubic-centimeter) graduated receiving flask, thermometers for measuring the temperature of the oil sample and of the oil bath, and a timing device.

The oil to be tested is strained and poured into the oil tube. The tube is surrounded by the constant-temperature oil bath. When the oil sample is at the correct temperature, the cork is pulled from the lower end of the tube and the sample flows through the orifice and into the graduated receiving flask. The time (in seconds) required for the oil to fill the receiving flask to the 60-cc mark is noted.

The viscosity of the oil is expressed by indicating three things: first, the number of seconds required for 60 cubic centimeters of oil to flow into the receiving flask; second, the type of orifice used; and third, the temperature of the oil sample at the time the viscosity determination is made. For example, suppose that a sample of lubricating oil is heated to 125°F and that 170 seconds are required for 60-cc of the sample of flow through a Saybolt Universal orifice and into the receiving flask. The viscosity of this oil is said to be 170 seconds Saybolt Universal at 125°F. This is usually expressed in shorter form as 170 SSU at 125°F (or 20 weight oil.)

Other oils have other temperatures that are used for obtaining Saybolt Universal viscosities. Thus, it is important that the temperature be included in the statement of viscosity.

Ignition Quality

The ignition quality of a diesel fuel is its ability to ignite when it is injected into the compressed air within the engine cylinders. Ignition quality is measured by the CETANE RATING of the fuel. A cetane number is obtained by comparing the ignition quality of a given diesel fuel with that of a reference fuel of known cetane number in a test engine. This reference fuel is a mixture of alphamethylnapthalene, which is difficult to ignite alone, and cetane, which

12

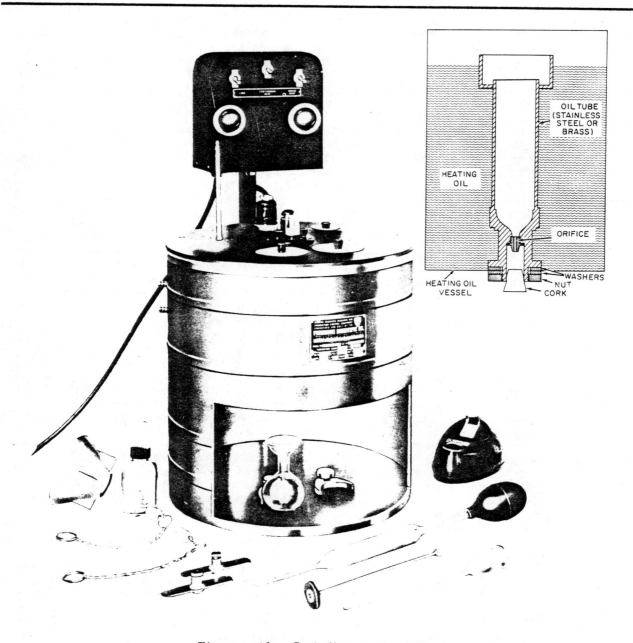

OIL TUBE (STAINLESS STEEL OR BRASS)

HEATING OIL

ORIFICE

HEATING OIL VESSEL

WASHERS

NUT

CORK

Figure 10. — Saybolt viscosimeter.

will ignite readily at temperatures and pressures comparable to those in the cylinders of a diesel engine. The cetane rating indicates the percentage of cetane in a reference fuel which will just match the ignition quality of the fuel being tested. The higher cetane numbers indicate more efficient fuels. The large slow diesels can use a 30 cetane fuel, but the high speed diesels must use at least a 40 cetane fuel, while some require as high as a 60 cetane fuel.

The ignition quality of a diesel-fuel depends also on its FLASH POINT and its FIRE POINT. The flast point is the temperature to which the fuel vapors must be heated to flash or ignite. The minimum flash point for diesel fuel is 150°

F. A fuel having too low a flash point is dangerous both to handle and to store.

The fire point is that temperature at which the fuel vapors will continue to burn after being ignited. It is usually 10 to 70 degrees higher than the flash point.

You will sometimes hear knocks in diesel engines. They are believed to be caused by the rapid burning of the fuel that accumulates in the delay period between injection and ignition. This delay is known as IGNITION LAG or IGNITION DELAY. When the fuel is injected into the cylinders, it must vaporize and be heated to the flash point to start combustion. The lag between vaporization and flash point depends upon the ignition quality of the fuel and the speed of the engine and its compression ratio. In high speed engines the delay varies from 0.0012 to 0.0018 of a second. Ignition lag decreases with the increase in engine speed because of a swifter air movement in the cylinders that makes the injected fuel heat better.

LUBRICANTS

A lubricant is a substance, usually a thin film of oil, used to reduce friction. There are three types of kinetic friction: sliding friction, rolling friction, and fluid friction. Sliding friction exists when the surface of one solid body is moved across the surface of another solid body. Rolling friction exists when a curved body such as a cylinder or a sphere rolls upon a flat or curved surface. Fluid friction is the resistance to motion exhibited by a fluid.

Fluid friction exists because of the cohesion between particles of the fluid and the adhesion of fluid particles to the object or medium which is tending to move the fluid. If a paddle is used to stir a fluid, for example, the cohesive forces between the molecules of the fluid tend to hold the molecules together and thus prevent motion of the fluid. At the same time, the adhesive forces of the molecules of the fluid cause the fluid to adhere to the paddle and thus create friction between the paddle and the fluid. Cohesion is the molecular attraction between particles that tends to hold a substance or a body together; adhesion is the molecular attraction between particles that tends to cause unlike surfaces to stick together. From the point of view of lubrication, adhesion is the property of a lubricant that causes it to stick (or adhere) to the parts being lubricated; cohesion is the property which holds the lubricant together and enables it to resist breakdown under pressure.

Besides reducing friction and wear, lubricants act as COOLING AGENTS, absorbing heat from the surfaces over which they are spread. This is true particularly of engine oil, which carries heat to the engine sump, where it is dissipated. The water circulating through an oil cooler also helps to reduce this heat (not all engines have oil coolers).

Lubricants are also used as SEALING agents. They fill the tiny openings between moving parts, cushioning them against damage and distortion from extreme heat.

Lubricants are also important as CLEANING AGENTS. Any grit and dirt finding their way into the engine parts often are removed by the lubricants before damage can result. Foreign matter found in old oils and greases in the bottom of the crankcase is evidence of the cleansing quality of lubricants. Some lubricants have chemicals added to make them better cleaners.

The high temperatures, speeds, and cylinder pressures of modern engines have made necessary better grades of lubricating oils. To increase efficiency, certain chemicals, called ADDITIVES, are put into oils. Additives are resistive agents which are used against oxidation and other kinds of metal deterioration. Oil which contains additives specifically designed to help clean the piston rings and other parts of the engine as it lubricates is known as DETERGENT OIL.

It is especially important for you to keep up with the latest developments in lubricants as presented in Navy and other technical publications. Your chief will tell you where you can get this information.

Types of Lubricants and Their Uses

Oils and greases are the two general types of lubricants. The modern high-speed gasoline or diesel engine must be properly lubricated with the proper grades and types of lubricating oils and greases. Present-day refining methods have produced lubricating oils and greases with certain special qualities. In engines operating at high speeds and temperatures, these oils do a better job than ordinary oils can do. Engines operating at low speeds or in cold weather may require an oil with other special qualities.

Greases are used where it is difficult to keep oil in place and where the lubricant is subjected to varying pressures. In some cases, greases are used when centrifugal forces tend to throw the lubricant from moving parts. This is especially true in gear boxes and wheel bearings.

OILS. — Lubricating oils serve four purposes: (1) prevent metal-to-metal contact in moving parts of mechanisms, (2) help carry heat away from the engine, (3) clean the engine parts as they are lubricated, and (4) form a seal between moving parts. Moving parts that do not have enough oil will melt, fuse, or seize after a very short period of engine operation. All gears and accessory drives, as well as other moving parts of the engine subject to friction, must be bathed in oil at all times.

We have seen that viscosity is the resistance of a liquid against flow. It is the most important property of a lubricating oil. A lubricant of high viscosity spreads very slowly. You have heard of car owners using a HEAVY oil in summer and changing to LIGHT oil in winter. The heavy oil used in summer becomes too sluggish in cold weather, while the light oil used in winter flows too easily in hot weather. An oil used in any engine must flow freely and have enough body to resist friction between moving engine parts; it must pass readily through all oil lines and spread effectively over all surfaces that require lubrication.

The temperature of an oil affects its viscosity. The higher the temperature, the lower the viscosity. On a cold morning, the high viscosity or stiffness of the lubricating oil makes an engine hard to turn over.

The viscosity of an oil is figured by the number of seconds which pass while a certain volume flows through a small opening or hole of a definite diameter at a given temperature. The greater the number of seconds, the higher the viscosity. The Society of Automotive Engineers (S.A.E.) has standardized a code of numbers to indicate the viscosity of lubricating oils. You will be using military symbols for these lubricating oils, which are expressed in four digits, as indicated in Table 1. The last three digits indicate the viscosity in number of seconds required for 60 cubic centimeters of oil to flow through a standard opening at a given temperature. The first digit indicates the class and type of lubricating oil. You will use only the lubricant recommended for the particular engine which you service and lubricate. It is advisable to check with your chief from time to time for discontinued and new stocks and changed designations or specification numbers.

Oil is a mixture of many slightly different compounds, and therefore does not have a definite freezing point, but it does thicken as it cools. In order to determine the usefulness of an oil in cold weather, it is tested for its POUR POINT, which is the lowest temperature at which the oil will still flow. The pour point in which you will be interested is the lowest temperature at which the oil on the cylinder walls and bearings will permit the engine to be turned.

While the flash point and the fire point of an oil do not affect its lubricating qualities, they are useful in determining the amount of volatile fluids or compounds in the oil. As you learned concerning diesel oil, the flash point is the temperature at which vapors will ignite, but not sustain a flame. The flash point of a lubricating oil for your entire engine must range from 300°F to 500°F to keep the oil from vaporizing too readily in the crankcase and to make it withstand the heat of the engine. It is used also to determine the fire hazard in shipping and storing the lubricant.

Again, as you previously learned, the fire point is the temperature at which vapors given off continue to burn when ignited. Both the flash point and the fire point must be taken into consideration in the blending of an oil of proper viscosity for the type and condition of the engine in which it is to be used.

From the day that fresh oil is put into the engine crankcase, it gradually begins to lose its effectiveness because of dilution and contamination from engine operation. Gasoline or diesel fuel may dribble into the crankcase oil. Water and sludge also may accumulate. Carbon, gum acids, and dust in the air entering the engine (in the air-fuel mixture) all reduce the effectiveness of any lubricant. It is because of this accumulation of foreign matter that manufacturers recommend regular oil changes, and that regular lubrication is so important in preventive maintenance.

GREASES. — Greases are compounds of oil and soap. The soaps used are not ordinary laundry soaps but animal fats mixed with certain chemicals. The chief purpose of the soap is to provide a body or carrier for the oil that actually does the lubricating.

Grease is used where oil is impractical or unsatisfactory due to centrifugal forces, loads, temperatures or exposure. For instance, it maintains a film at high engine speed and temperature, or when the equipment is idle for long periods of time.

The chemicals in the grease classify it for a particular purpose or use. CHASSIS GREASES have a lime, sodium, or an aluminum soap base. Chassis greases are distinguished by their shiny, transparent appearance, and are used as a pressure gum lubricant for chassis, U-joints, track rollers, and low temperature ball bearings.

CUP GREASE, or WATER-PUMP GREASE, is a lime-base grease to which water or moisture is added to keep the soap from separating from the oil. The moisture gives the grease a somewhat cloudy appearance, and it will evaporate at a temperature equal to that of boiling water. Lime base greases are not recommended for parts subjected to high temperature. These greases are recommended when moisture resistance is required, and are satisfactory for water pumps and marine stuffing boxes.

WHEEL BEARING or FIBROUS GREASES have a sodium or mixed soap base. These greases only appear fibrous, for there are no actual fibers in them. They are recommended for wheel bearings because they stick or cling to parts. Since they are not water resistant, they can be used only on protected parts.

CABLE GREASE (wire rope and exposed gear grease) is a sticky black oil used to lubricate chains and wire ropes.

The black, tar-like sticky mass called CRATER COMPOUND is used to grease sliding surfaces and exposed gears on heavy duty construction equipment. It is applied by hand or with a brush and cannot be squeezed from between the gear teeth or the sliding surfaces. You will find a can of this grease on nearly every shovel or crane used.

Some form of dry lubricant such as GRAPHITE POWDER is available in the shop, to lubricate small parts and door locks, where a liquid would run off or otherwise be undesirable.

Petroleum refiners have developed greases to meet special lubrication requirements of modern machinery and equipment. Table 2 lists and describes the kinds of greases and their uses for proper maintenance.

CONTAMINATION OF PRODUCTS

A contaminated product is one to which has been added some material not normally present such as dirt, rust, water, or another petroleum product. Such admixture may modify the usual qualities of the product permanently or add new and undesirable characteristics. In either case, the contaminated product may be unsuitable for its intended use. Contamination may result from accident, inability or neglect or follow prescribed procedures, gross carelessness, or sabotage. In most instances contamination of a product can be detected by its unusual appearance, color, gravity, or odor.

Dirt

The causes for the presence of sand, clay, or loam in appreciable quantity in petroleum products should be investigated at once and remedial action taken. It may be the result of carelessness or of sabotage. Most commonly it is the result of inadequate cleaning and inspection of tanks or containers, or the use of muddy water to flush pipelines.

In light fuels such as gasoline, in cans or drums, dirt settles in a few hours. The clear fuel may then be drawn off and the bottom (4 to 10 inches) recovered by filtration through a dry chamois. An alternative is to decant the fuel into larger containers for further settling by pouring off the fuel without disturbing the sediment in the bottom of the container. In bulk tanks the settling may require 12 to 24 hours. The clear fuel may then be run off to clean storage and the bottom layer passed through gasoline filters, if available, or downgraded. Tanks and other containers should be thoroughly cleaned before reusing. In heavier fuels such as diesel oils or JP-5 jet fuel, settling is much less satisfactory. Filtration is recommended if practicable. Otherwise it is usually necessary to downgrade the product. In the case of lube oils and greases, no remedial action can be taken. The product must be downgraded.

Rust

Rust is the common name for the product of corrosion which is formed when unprotected iron or some steel surfaces are subjected to prolonged contact with water or moist air. It is brittle and powders readily. It is insoluble in water and in petroleum products but may form troublesome suspensions because of turbulent flow in pipelines, the churning action produced while pumping into storage tanks, or the rough

Table 1.—Military and Commerical Designation for Gear and Lubricating Oils Used in Equipment Maintenance

General Description	Military Designation and Specification Number	Typical Commercial Designation	Uses
Gear oil. . . . . . Containing extreme pressure (EP) additives to maintain lubrication under extreme pressure conditions.	Lubricant, Gear, Universal, MIL-L-10324. FSN 9150-259-5443.	E.P. Hypoid Gear Lubricant. Universal Gear Lubricant for very cold climates.	For all gear lubrication including transmission, differentials, hypoid gears, tractor final drives, and steering gear mechanisms in cold climates when the prevailing temperature is below 0° F.
Gear oil. . . . . Containing extreme pressure (EP) additives to maintain lubrication under extreme pressure conditions.	Lubricant, Gear, Universal, MIL-L-2105. FSN 9150-577-5842.	SAE 80 EP Hypoid or Universal Gear Lubricant. MA 1327	As above except that it is an SAE 80 gear lubricant for use where the prevailing temperature is between 0° and 32° F.
	FSN 9150-577-5845.	SAE 90 EP Hypoid or Universal Gear Lubricant. MA 1328	As above except that it is an SAE 90 gear lubricant for use where the prevailing temperature is above 0° F.
Mineral Gear Oil, SAE 140. NO ADDITIVES.	Military Symbol 5190. MIL-L-2105. FSN 9150-577-5848.	SAE 140 Mineral Gear Oil. Steam Cylinder Oil. MA 1329	For use in tractor transmissions and final drives only in tropical areas. There are no extreme pressure chemical additives in this oil. DO NOT mix with extreme pressure lubricants. DO NOT use in hypoid gear drives such as truck or passenger vehicle differentials.
SAE-10 Heavy Duty Lubricating Oil.	Military Symbol 9110. FSN 9150-231-9039.	Gasoline and Diesel Engine Oil, SAE-10 and SAE-10 W Grades.	For crankcase lubrication in both gasoline and diesel engines requiring an SAE-10 or SAE-10 W oil and for general purpose lubrication.
SAE-20 Heavy Duty Lubricating Oil.	Military Symbol 9170. FSN 9150-231-6651.	Gasoline and Diesel Engine Oil, SAE-20 Grade.	For crankcase lubrication in both gasoline and diesel engines requiring an SAE-20 oil and for general purpose lubrication.
SAE-30 Heavy Duty Lubricating Oil.	Military Symbol 9250. FSN 9150-231-6655.	Gasoline and Diesel Engine Oil, SAE-30 Grade. MB 1702	For crankcase lubrication in both gasoline and diesel engines requiring an SAE-30 oil and for general purpose lubrication.
SAE-40 Heavy Duty Lubricating Oil.	Military Symbol 9370. FSN 9150-912-9552.	Gasoline and Diesel Engine Oil, SAE-40 Grade.	For crankcase lubrication in both gasoline and diesel engines requiring an SAE-40 oil and for general purpose lubrication.

Table 1.—Military and Commerical Designation for Gear and Lubricating Oils Used in Equipment Maintenance—Continued

General Description	Military Designation and Specification Number	Typical Commercial Designation	Uses
SAE-50 Heavy Duty Lubricating Oil.	Military Symbol 9500. FSN 1950-231-9043.	Gasoline and Diesel Engine Oil, SAE-50 Grade. MB 1722	For crankcase lubrication in both gasoline and diesel engines requiring an SAE-50 oil and for general purpose lubrication.
Medium VI Mineral Oil SAE-50. No additives.	Military Symbol 3100. FSN 9150-223-8893.	Mineral Oil SAE-50	For lubrication of certain 2-stroke cycle gasoline engines where prescribed. Mixed with fuel in specified proportions such as outboard motorboat engines. For general purpose lubrication.
Hydraulic Transmission Fluid, Type C-1	EO—Series 3 or MIL-L-45199A. Grade 10. FSN 9150-680-1103.	Lubricating Oil High Output.	For hydraulic systems and certain transmission and converter units as prescribed by the manufacturer.

handling of small containers. Rust is a commonly occurring source of contamination when disused pipelines or containers are employed without proper cleaning. Its prevention in small containers—where it is most likely to occur—is best accomplished by thorough cleaning and subsequent rinsing of the container with a prescribed rust-preventive type oil or solution which will cling to the metal surface in a thin layer and provide temporary protection until the container can be filled with the product to be stored. While empty, the containers should be stored upside down. Active pipelines and large storage facilities do not normally permit the accumulation of rust in appreciable quantity. Rust may be removed from gasoline and heavier fuels by the same methods employed in removing dirt from these products.

Mill-Scale

Mill-scale is a magnetic product formed on iron and some steel surfaces during the manufacturing process. It is largely responsible for the blue-black appearance of such surfaces. It has been observed as a very serious contaminant in bulk products pumped through new pipes during the first few days or weeks of use. The scale is brittle and cracks readily. Corrosion begins at these cracks and proceeds to spread under the scale causing it to flake off. The scale is then carried along by the oil flow and is broken up still further before it reaches terminal storage. Here it may remain suspended for days. Settling is not, therefore, a satisfactory method of elimination. The scale is not removed completely by segregators and consequently, screens are quickly choked. Filtering of such stocks is recommended.

Water

In bulk storage, water can very often be a reason for fuel contamination. Water is sometimes employed as a bottom, to a depth of a few inches, to underlie light products such as gasolines and jet fuels. However, the use of water bottoms should be avoided if at all possible, and only employed when authorized by proper technical authority. It is sometimes used to separate and prevent mixing of products when two products, such as motor gasoline and

Table 2.—Military and Commerical Designations for Greases Used in Equipment Maintenance

General Description	Military Designation and Specification Number	Typical Commercial Designation	Uses
Grease, Chasis—Lime, soda or aluminum soap base grease.	Lubricant, General Mil-G-10924 Mil Sym GAA FSN 9150-530-7369	Chassis Grease, Cup Grease, Pressure Gun Grease, No. 1—Soft.	For general use as a pressure gun lubricant, particularly chassis, universal joints, track rollers, ball bearings operating below 150° F. Lime and aluminum soap base grease types are water resistant.
Grease, Wheel Bearing Soda or mixed soap base grease.	Lubricant, General Purpose, No. 2 (Wheel-Bearing-Chassis Lubricant—WB). VV-G-632 Type B, Grade 2. FSN 9150-531-6971.	Wheel Bearing Grease, No. 2—Medium.	For wheel bearings, ball bearings, and as a pressure gun lubricant when operating temperatures are expected to be above 150° F. DO NOT USE TO GREASE UNIVERSAL JOINTS OR OTHER PARTS HAVING NEEDLE BEARINGS. Not water resistant.
Grease, Ball and Roller Bearing Soda or mixed soap base grease.	Lubricant, Ball and Roller Bearing. Mil-G-18709. FSN 9150-249-0908.	Ball and Roller Bearing Grease, BRB.	BRB and G-18709 suitable for ball and roller bearing lubrication, especially in electric motors and generators and clutch pilot bearings. Not water resistant.
Grease—Water Pump Lime soap base grease.	Lubricant, Water-Pump, No. 4. VV-G-632 Type A, Grade 4. FSN 9150-235-5504.	Water-Pump Grease, No. 4—Hard.	For gland type water-pumps of some engines not equipped with factory lubricated and sealed water pumps. Very water resistant.
Lubricant, Exposed Gear, Chain, and Wire Rope Sticky, viscous, black, residual oil.	Lubricant, Chain and Wire Rope. Mil-G-18458. FSN 9150-530-6814.	Exposed Gear Chain and Wire Rope Lubricant. Gear Grease. Wire Rope Grease No. 2.	For greasing cable, open gears or any open mechanism requiring rough lubrication. Usually heated before applying. Grade B is intended for use in temperate or warm weather and is suitable for open-air or under-water conditions. Not for cables in contact with earth.
		As above, except that it is No. 3 or heavy duty type.	As above except that Grade C is for use in hot weather or for hard service and is suitable for open-air or under-water conditions.

aviation gasoline, are to be pumped through a pipeline, one after the other. Again, this should be avoided if possible as there are better means for segregation of products. The legitimate and necessary uses of water provide ample opportunities for the contamination of light products unless they are controlled by strict adherence to standard operating procedures. Fortunately, water suspended in light products such as gasoline separates rapidly on standing; less rapidly in diesel oil and JP-5 jet fuel. In cold weather this settling may be delayed by the formation of ice crystals, which are lighter than water droplets. In suspension, these crystals may clog filters, fuel lines, or jets in equipment. The most effective precaution against water contamination is to ensure delivery of a well-settled product through a dry line into a dry container. In cold weather, even a small amount of water can cause the freezing of bottom outlet valves in rail tank cars and tank trucks. In the case of packaged products, water may become a contaminant through the use of open or damaged containers, through improper storage and handling methods, and by the breathing which normally occurs in drums and cans. (Breathing is the reverse of vaporization and is caused by a drop in temperature. In breathing, cooled vapors condense to liquids, the interior pressure of the storage tank or container decreases, and air is sucked into the tank or container.)

Water contamination of fuels supplied to consumers in drums or cans can be avoided, when the turnover is rapid, by the application of prescribed methods of inspection, storage, and handling. However, long-term storage in drums, (strategic reserve stocks) cannot fail to result in some contamination. The condensation of some water from the moist air sucked in during the night is inevitable since this water settles and, therefore, is not expelled with product vapors during the heat of the day. During several weeks of storage, this water accumulates in surprisingly large amounts. Not only does it constitute direct contamination, which may have very undesirable consequences if transferred to equipment, but it is the cause of serious additional contamination by rust, and increases container maintenance. For this reason, periodic technical inspection is required and provision must be made for the regular replacement of such stocks at relatively frequent intervals. The length of intervals is determined by climatic and other conditions. Accumulated water can best be removed by decantation, settling, and refilling. Lacking time

or facilities for this, a small pump may be employed to remove the lower layers from individual containers.

The most effective and proper protection for lubricants is to keep them well covered, preferably in inside storage. Should damaged containers permit water to contaminate engine or gear oils, the water may remove some of the essential additives. Even more undesirable is the fact that water tends to emulsify in the oil and does not settle out, thus decreasing effective lubricating action. Water can be poured off from greases. When this is done, about an inch of surface grease should also be removed. After removal, the surface grease should be burned or buried.

Commingling of Products

Commingling of products may result from inadequate cleansing of lines or containers; from the use of unmarked or improperly marked containers; and from the mishandling of manifolds. In such cases it can be minimized by supervision sufficient to ensure strict application of the prescribed petroleum handling procedures. Commingling may also result from leaks in tanks or valves aboard tankers, and from leaky valves or insufficient protective facilities in shore installations. These sources can be minimized by proper inspection and maintenance procedures. Nevertheless, serious contamination of one product by another can and does occur occasionally in field operations. This is one of the most compelling reasons for the continuous inspection procedures and the routine testing programs prescribed by the military departments.

Commingling can be negligible or serious depending upon the product contaminated, the contaminating agent, and the amount of contamination. Some of the more important serious effects are:

1. Loss of power in fuels.
2. Increase in volatility (producing a fire or explosion hazard in kerosene or diesel fuels).
3. Increase in gum content.
4. Formation of heavy sludge.

III. SAFETY IN HANDLING AND STORAGE OF PETROLEUM PRODUCTS

Although the handling of petroleum products presents many hazards, both bulk and packaged products can be handled safely and with remarkable freedom from accident if proper precautionary measures are taken. All personnel involved with the receipt, storage, issue, and use of flammable and combustible petroleum products must be familiar with and observe applicable safety precautions.

Precautionary measures must be taken to prevent fire and explosion when handling any petroleum product. The degree of hazard involved depends on the properties of a given product. Therefore, for safe handling purposes, petroleum products are divided into groups or classes according to the temperature at which the product will give off flammable vapors.

Any material which can be ignited easily and which will burn with unusual rapidity is said to be flammable. (The terms flammable and inflammable are identical in meaning, but the former is preferred since the prefix in suggests non flammable.)

All petroleum products, being composed of carbon and hydrogen, will burn and are therefore combustible materials. However, classification for safe handling purposes distinguishes products according to their tendency to burn.

Combustible liquids, according to the National Fire Protection Association (NFPA) Standards, are those liquids having flash points at or above 140°F and below 200°F.

Flammable liquids, according to the NFPA Standards, include all liquid petroleum fuels which give off flammable vapors below temperatures of 140°F.

Volatile products are products which tend to vaporize; that is, give off flammable vapors at comparatively low temperatures are said to be volatile. Because volatile products such as gasoline and JP-4 jet fuels will give off sufficient vapors to be flammable at relatively low temperatures, they are the most hazardous of all petroleum products to handle. For example, gasoline has a flash point of about -45° and JP-4 jet fuel has a flash point slightly higher, while crude oil has a flash point of about 60°F. This varies, however, according to the source of the crude oil. Volatile products such as gasoline and JP-4 jet fuel are normally handled at atmospheric temperatures above -45°F and, therefore, give off sufficient vapors to flash or

burn at all times. Products which give off flammable vapors only above 100°F and are relatively nonvolatile are relatively safe to handle at ordinary temperatures and pressures. Such petroleum products as kerosene, JP-5 jet fuel, diesel and light and heavy fuel oils are included in this category.

It is noted, however, that if products such as kerosene, JP-5 jet fuel, diesels and fuel oils are handled at elevated temperatures they are just as hazardous as the volatile products. For example, kerosene, which has a flash point of about 110°F will not ignite at ordinary atmospheric temperatures, but if it is heated above 100°F will give off sufficient flammable vapors to burn or explode. All products which have a flash point above 100°F when heated to temperatures equal to or higher than their flash point, should be treated as volatile products with respect to fire and explosion hazards.

Some precautionary measures to be strictly observed when handling petroleum products are listed below. Most of these precautions apply to the handling of any flammable or volatile product at ordinary temperature, and higher flash or less volatile products at high temperature.

1. Reducing Or Controlling The Discharge Of Vapors

a. Take care that no spills occur.

b. Avoid spills from overflow when loading storage tanks by gaging tanks prior to loading.

c. Never neglect leaks. Make frequent inspections for leaks in tank seams, tank shells, and pipe joints.

d. If spills or leaks occur, clean them up immediately. Soaked ground should be washed with water or covered with sand or dry earth. The area should be policed until flammable vapor has been eliminated.

e. When temperatures are excessively high, cool storage tanks by sprinkling, or by playing water over them.

f. Keep containers for volatile products, whether empty or full, closed tightly.

g. Beware of empty fuel containers.

h. Ensure proper ventilation of all enclosed spaces in which vapors may accumulate.

2. Eliminating Sources Of Accidental Ignition

a. Do not smoke.

b. Do not carry "strike anywhere" matches or automatic lighters that open and light with a single motion.

c. Do not perform any mechanical work or repair involving hot work such as burning, cutting, or welding, unless a permit is issued by proper authority.

d. Inspect electrical apparatus frequently and correct any condition likely to cause sparking.

e. Open switches and pull fuses before work is done on electrical equipment.

f. Shut off gasoline tank truck engines during the entire period of filling or discharging unless the truck is designed for engine operation, to drive transfer pumps through a power take-off.

g. Ground flammable fuel hose nozzle to the tank before starting the flow of fuel. Maintain this bond throughout the filling operation.

h. Never load or unload volatile or flammable products during electrical storms.

i. Use only self-closing metal receptacles for discarding oily waste or rags and dispose of such collections daily.

j. Never use volatile petroleum products such as gasoline for any cleaning purpose.

k. Keep gage tape in contact with gage hatch during gaging operations.

l. Immediately remove any clothing which has become soaked with fuels.

3. Safety Precautions For Handling JP-4 Fuel:

In addition to the safety precautions required for handling all volatile fuels, Grade JP-4 fuel, because of its tendency to accumulate and discharge static electricity and its low vapor pressure, requires additional handling precautions. Like other volatile fuels, JP-4 still requires a source of ignition. Unlike the other volatile fuels, the static electricity generated in pumping, transferring and loading JP-4 is an inherrent source of ignition which requires careful handling to control. JP-4 fuel is unique in that its rate of vaporization under most handling conditions will create an atmosphere (vapor/air) well within the explosive range, within the tank above the liquid surface. The atmosphere within a fixed roof tank storing gasoline will normally be too rich to be ignited or to burn within the tank, but in the case of JP-4, any ignition at gaging hatches, or vents will travel into the tank and cause a violent combustion (explosion). This hazard is not normally present in the case of Grade JP-5 fuel because of its relatively high flash point (140°F). To minimize the generation and a accumulation of static electric charge in JP-4 fuel, the following procedures and/or precautions are recommended:

a. Do not use overhead fill lines which permit a free fall of product through the air.

b. The entrance of air into fill lines should be minimized or eliminated if practicable.

c. Where feasible the storage of JP-4 in concrete tanks or other poor electrical conducting materials should be avoided.

When handling petroleum products, care must be taken to ensure they do not become contaminated with foreign matter. Since all petroleum products will burn, fire is an ever present hazard. The degree of fire hazard increases as the volatility of the product increases.

Inhaling gasoline vapors may cause headaches, dizziness, nausea, or even unconsciousness. If any of these symptoms are noticed among men handling gasoline or working in an area where gasoline has been spilled, the men should leave the area at once. If anyone has been overcome, he should receive immediate medical attention.

Gasoline may cause severe burns if allowed to remain in contact with the skin, particularly under soaked clothing or gloves. Clothing or shoes through which gasoline has soaked should be removed at once. Gasoline should be washed from the skin with soap and water. Repeated contact with gasoline removes the protective oils from the skin and causes drying, roughening, chapping, and cracking and, in some cases, infections of the skin. Rubber gloves should be worn as protection by persons handling petroleum products.

If gasoline gets into a person's eyes, first aid should be given immediately. Fresh water may be applied, and medical attention should be secured.

If a person swallows gasoline by accident, first aid should be given immediately. Giving the victim warm salty water to induce vomiting is an effective aid. Medical attention should be secured promptly.

Slipping and falling are common accidents which occur when handling petroleum products. This danger is particularly grave while climbing to and from loading racks, storage tanks, or stacks of drums or cans. Tools, pieces of lumber, and other objects should not be left lying where they may cause accidents.

22

On a hot day, gasoline vapors mixed with air may be flammable for a distance of 20 feet from an open container. By using underground tanks there will be less chance of a fire or an explosion, and less gas will be lost by evaporation. Areas near gasoline storage tanks should ALWAYS BE WELL POSTED WITH WARNING SIGNS.

Gasoline storage tanks should be placed underground and covered with at least 3 or 4 feet of earth. The tanks must be equipped with vent pipes which extend well above the ground (6 to 8 feet) so that the vapors may spread and disappear. (See fig. 11.)

Diesel fuel is not as volatile, flammable, nor as dangerous to handle as gasoline. But it will burn, and in closed unventilated places, diesel vapors can be explosive.

Diesel fuel is generally not stored in the same way as gasoline. Figure 12 shows a typical diesel fuel storage tank. The tank is generally placed above ground on a raised platform. The platform should be high enough to permit the fueling of equipment from the tank by gravity flow. The tank must be provided with an air vent at the top and a drain cock at the lowest point. The outlet for the fuel should be at least 6 inches from the bottom of the tank, so that any water and dirt which have accumulated and settled in the bottom will not be drained into the fuel tanks of the equipment being serviced. The water and sediment that collect in the bottom of the tanks should be drained off daily. When you fill a diesel fuel storage tank, remember to leave enough room for expansion of the fuel. Lubricating oil and greases are furnished in various sizes of containers. More lubricant is wasted because it has become contaminated than for any other cause. All containers should be clearly marked as to their contents and dates received. The lubricants that have been in stock the longest should be used first. Make sure that all openings of lubricant containers are properly secured. This will decrease the chances of lubricants becoming contaminated.

IV. FILTERS

In discussing diesel fuel, it was emphasized that it must be clean for proper diesel engine operation. So important is clean fuel, that besides the precautions observed in handling and storing diesel fuel, manufacturers have built fuel strainers and filters into the fuel systems or diesel engines.

FUEL OIL FILTERS

In addition to a metal strainer, most diesel-fuel systems also contain a filter to remove any remaining small particles of dirt that might clog the injectors. Fuel-oil filters are manufactured in various models by a number of manufacturers. All fuel entering the injectors first passes through the filter elements. The filter elements are made of cotton fiber or mineral wool and glass cloth. After continued use, these filters will become packed with dirt filtered from the fuel, and the flow of fuel to the engine will be reduced to a point where the engine ceases to function properly or stops. Most types of heavy equipment have fuel pressure gages which will indicate when filters are dirty. Filter elements are easily removed and should be replaced with new elements when they start to restrict the flow of fuel to the engine.

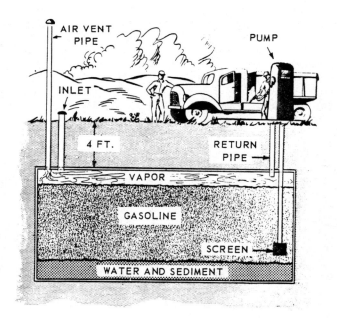

Figure 11. — Underground gasoline storage tank.

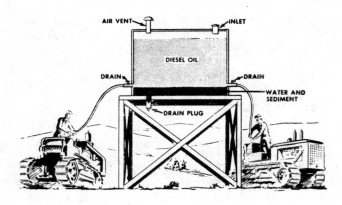

Figure 12. — Storage tank for diesel fuel.

LUBRICATING OIL
FILTERS

Most internal combustion engines are equipped with an oil filter. This device filters out the dust, dirt, and grit that enter the oil during operation of the engine.

Construction equipment lubricating oil filters (fig. 13) contain a filtering element for their filtering action. When this filtering element is saturated with solid particles, it ceases to function. It is good practice to replace the element with a new one every time the crankcase is drained and new oil is added. By such replacement you are assured of clean oil and a minimum of wear on engine parts.

The three types of oil filter systems used on automotive engines are the bypass, full-flow, and shunt types. The bypass type of oil filter is bracket mounted to the cylinder head or manifolds with connecting oil lines to the engine. The oil from the oil pump passes through the oil filter and then to the crankcase in the bypass system. The full-flow type of oil filter is integral with the engine. The oil is directed under pressure through the filter and then to the engine bearings. When the oil is too cold to circulate through the filter in the full-flow system, a bypass valve directs the oil around the filter element. The shunt type filters only a portion of the oil at a time, as does the bypass system, but the oil which is filtered is passed directly to the engine bearings.

Bypass systems use three types of filters. They are the throw-away type (fig. 14), the screw-on type of throw-away filter (fig. 15), and the replaceable element type of filter (fig. 16). The full-flow and shunt systems use the replaceable element type of the screw-on type of throw-away filter. A replaceable element for a full-flow type filter is shown in figure 17.

The throw-away type of oil filter is replaced as a complete unit. You have to disconnect the oil line fittings at the filter. Detach the filter from its bracket and remove the brass fitting from its filter housing. Throw away the filter. Place a bolt or plug into the brass fitting when you are removing or installing it. Brass is malleable (easily bent) and may be crushed by excessive wrench pressure.

The screw-on, throw-away type filter is also replaced as a complete unit. You unscrew

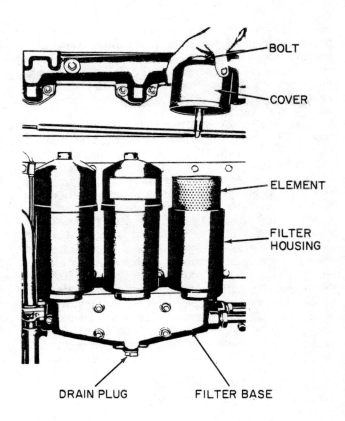

Figure 13. — Lubricating oil filter for construction equipment.

the filter from the base by hand and throw the filter away. Wipe the base clean with a cloth and screw a new filter onto the base by hand, tightening at least half a turn after the gasket contacts the base. Fill the crankcase to the full mark on the dipstick with the proper grade and weight of oil. Start the engine and observe the oil pressure and check for leaks around the oil filter. Stop the engine and add oil to the full level if needed.

To service replaceable element oil filters, you remove the fastening bolt, lift off the cover or remove the filter shell. Remove the gasket and throw it away. When removing the oil filter of the full-flow or shunt type, place a pan under the filter to catch the oil. Take out the old element and throw it away. Throw away the gasket from the top and bottom of the center tube if they are present. Place a pan under the filter and remove the drain plug if the filter is used in the bypass system. Clean the inside of the filter shell and cover. Install metal supports

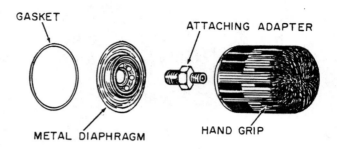

Figure 15.—Screw-on type of throw-away oil filter.

and a new bottom tube gasket. Insert a new element and a new top tube gasket. Insert a new cover or housing gasket (make sure that the gasket is completely seated in the recess). Replace the cover or housing and fasten the center bolt securely. Fill the crankcase to the full mark on the dip stick with the proper grade

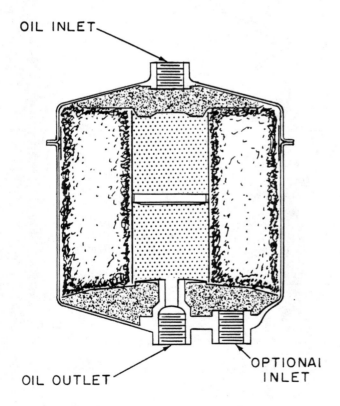

Figure 14.—Sealed type of throw-away oil filter.

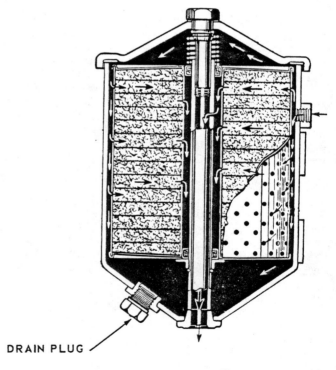

Figure 16.—Replaceable element type oil filter.

25

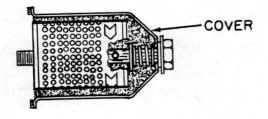

COVER

Figure 17. — Replaceable element, full-flow
type oil filter.

and weight of oil. Start and idle the engine.
Check the oil pressure immediately and inspect
the filter for oil leaks. Then stop the engine and
check the crankcase oil level and add oil to the
full mark. The final step in the procedure is to
mark the mileage on the sticker so that the
element of the oil filter will be replaced at the
proper interval.

DRY-TYPE AIR CLEANERS

The heavy duty dry-type air cleaner illustrated in figure 18 uses a replaceable element. Air enters the cleaner through the air intake cap and screen (1) which prevents chaff and
coarse dirt from getting into the air cleaner.
After passing through the adapter (3) and roto-
namic panel (4), the air is filtered as it passes
through the replaceable dry-type element (5)
and filter housing (6). The filtered air is then
drawn into the engine through the intake manifold.

OIL-BATH AIR CLEANER

The oil-bath air cleaner shown in figure
19 consists of main body, air intake cap,
screens, and oil reservoir. Air enters the intake cap and inlet screen (1) which prevent
large particles such as dirt, chaff, leaves, and
so forth, from entering the air cleaner. After
passing down the inlet pipe (2) to the center
oil reservoir (3), the air is deflected upward
through the screen (4), carrying drops of oil.
The oil absorbs dirt from the air as it passes
through the screen. The screen is sloped so
the air sweeps the dirt laden oil toward the
outside of the cleaner where it falls and re-
enters the oil reservoir. The clean filtered air
is then drawn into the engine through the intake
manifold pipe (5).

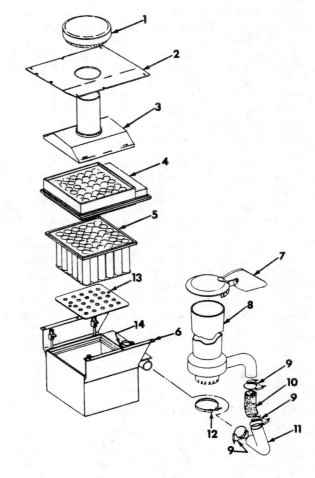

1. CAP, air intake.	8. ASPIRATOR.
2. PANEL, removeable.	9. CLAMP.
3. ADAPTER, intake.	10. HOSE.
4. PANEL, rotonamic.	11. ELBOW, exhaust.
5. ELEMENT, filter.	12. CLAMP, aspirator.
6. HOUSING, air cleaner.	13. PLATE, support.
7. CAP, weather.	14. GASKET.

Figure 18. — Heavy duty dry-type air cleaner.

V. ENVIRONMENTAL POLLUTION CONTROL

Environmental pollution is that condition which
results from the presence of chemical, physical
or biological agents in the air, water or soil

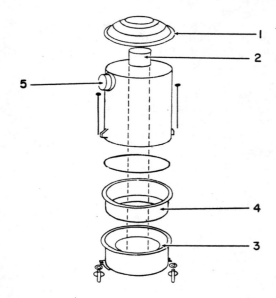

1. Intake cup and inlet screen.
2. Inlet pipe.
3. Center oil reservoir.
4. Screen.
5. Intake manifold pipe.

Figure 19. — Oil bath air cleaner.

which alter the natural environment. This causes an adverse effect on human health or comfort, fish and wildlife, other aquatic resources and plant life, and structures and equipment to the extent that economic loss is produced and re- creational opportunity is impaired. Pollution causes nylon hose to disintegrate, masonry to crumble, steel to corrode, and skies to darken. It also damages vegetation, causes illness, and results in the loss of countless work days.

AIR POLLUTION

As an EO, you should be aware of the con- ditions which cause air pollution when operat- ing equipment, and the efforts being made to minimize or correct these conditions.

When incomplete combustion occurs, unburned hydrocarbons and various other constituents in the basic fuel combine chemically to form some visible, noxious, and harmful byproducts which are emitted into the environment. Some of the fuel components and combustion products which

have an adverse effect on the air are carbon monoxide, particulate matter, sulfur, oxides, unburned hydrocarbons, nitrogen oxides, and lead.

CONTROLLING AIR POLLUTION

The most effective means of controlling air pollution caused by fuel combustion is to main- tain a well-tuned engine that provides an opti- mium fuel and oxygen mixture and proper tim- ing; this results in most efficient combustion. Another alternative, not always under control of an operator, is to use only the best grade of fuel available which contains low particulate matter, low water and sulfur content, and other contaminates. Automotive manufacturers now provide systems on engine to return "blowby" (unburned fuel) to the carburetor for combustion, i.e., a pollution control system. Long range research and development is underway in deve- loping systems to remove harmful constituents from engine exhausts, e.g., catalytic filter scrub- ber systems to remove oxides of sulfur and nitrogen, and others to remove lead.

WATER AND GROUND
POLLUTION

In addition to creating a fire hazard, oil and other fuel products pose many possible pollution threats when spilled on the water or ground. Oil products on the ground can infiltrate and contaminate ground water supplies or can be carried into surface water supplies with ground runoff due to rain. Oil products carried into storm or sanitary sewers pose potential ex- plosion hazards. Gasoline seeping into a sewer from a service station created an explosion which demolished several city blocks in a Chicago suburb

Oil on the water surface blocks the oxygen flow from the atmosphere into the water which results in less oxygen in the water for the fish and other aquatic organisms. Fish can be harmed by eating oil or smaller organisms that have eaten the oil. If the fish do not die from the oil coating their gills or from eating the oil, their flesh is tainted and they are no longer suitable for consumption by man. In addition to harming aquatic organisms and con- taminating water supplies, oil products foul boats, water front structures, beaches, and in general create an unsightly mess along the waterfront.

Of all the oil introduced in the world's waters, spent oils from highway vehicles accounted for 37 percent, or 2 million tons in 1969. This is the largest single source of oil pollution, ever greater than tankers (11 percent), other ships (10 percent), offshore oil production (2 percent), refineries and petrochemical plants (6 percent), industrial and all other vehicles (31 percent), and accidental spills (4 percent).

PREVENTIVE MEASURES FOR WATER AND GROUND POLLUTION

During automotive repair, drip pans and an absorbent material should be used to catch all unavoidable spills. Spilled oil or fuels should never be washed down a drain or sewer, unless an immediate fire hazard exists and an oil-water separator is present in the discharge line. Where spills are expected to occur (gasoline fill stands, etc.), absorbent material should be on hand. This material can be sprinkled on spilled oil or fuel, placed in a container, and disposed in a sanitary landfill or other non-polluting manner.

Spent crankcase oil, filters, contaminated fuel should be collected and disposed of in a non-polluting manner. Most naval activities collect and dispose of waste oil periodically through a contractor, by burning in a boiler plant, or reprocessing in an oil reclamation plant. Naval supply fuel farms usually have means to properly dispose of waste oils.

Open vehicle repair or maintenance areas located near water-courses or bodies of water should be landscaped and diked so spilled oil products cannot easily or directly flow into the nearby water.

DIESEL ENGINES

TROUBLESHOOTING

Anyone who has had experience analyzing troubles in gasoline engines, such as automobile engines, will find similarities between the procedures he has used and those described in this chapter. The mechanical similarity between gasoline and diesel engines dictates that many of their problems will be shared. The principal differences are the result of the diesel engine's greater size, fuel injection, use of superchargers, and application to a marine environment.

In this chapter we shall be concerned with troubles encountered in starting an engine and with troubles encountered after an engine is started. The troubles listed are chiefly of the kind that can be corrected without major overhaul or repair, and troubles that can be identified by erratic operation of the engine, by warnings given by the instruments, or by inspection of the engine parts and systems.

Keep in mind that the troubles we listed are general and may, or may not, apply to a particular diesel engine. When working with a specific engine, check the manufacturer's technical manual.

I. THE TROUBLESHOOTER

Complete failure of a power plant at a crucial moment may imperil all personnel. Even comparatively minor engine trouble, if not recognized and corrected as soon as possible, may develop into a major breakdown. Therefore, it is essential that every operator of an internal-combustion engine train himself to be a successful troubleshooter.

It may happen that an engine will continue to operate even when a serious casualty is imminent. However, if troubles are impending, there will probably be symptoms present, and the success of a troubleshooter depends partially upon his ability to recognize these symptoms when they occur. The good operator uses most of his senses to detect trouble symptoms. He may see, hear, smell, or feel the warning of trouble to come. Of course, common sense is also a requisite. Another factor upon which the success of a troubleshooter depends is his ability to locate the trouble after once deciding something is wrong with the equipment. Then he must be able to determine as rapidly as possible what corrective action must be taken. In learning to recognize and locate engine troubles, experience is the best teacher.

Instruments play an important part in the detection of engine troubles. The engine operator should read the instruments and record their indications regularly. If the recorded indications vary radically from those specified by engine operating instructions, it is a warning that the engine is not operating properly and that some type of corrective action must be taken. Familiarity with the specifications given in engine operating instructions is essential, especially those pertaining to temperatures, pressures and speeds. When instrument indications vary considerably from the specified values, the operator should know the probable effect on the engine. When variations occur in instrument indications, before taking any corrective action the operator should be sure that such variations are not the fault of the instrument. Instruments should be checked immediately when they are suspected of being inaccurate.

Periodic inspections are also essential in detecting engine troubles. Failure of visible parts, presence of smoke, or leakage of oil, fuel, or water can be discovered by such inspections. Cleanliness is probably one of the greatest aids in the detection of leakage.

When an engine is secured because of trouble, the procedure for repairing the casualty follows an established pattern, if the trouble has been diagnosed. If the location of the trouble is not known, it must be found. To inspect every part of an engine whenever a trouble occurs would be an almost endless task. The cause of a trouble can be found much more quickly if a systematic and logical method of inspection is followed. Generally speaking, a well-trained troubleshooter can isolate a trouble by identifying it with one of the engine systems. Once the trouble has been associated with a particular system, the next step is to trace out the system until you find the cause of the trouble. Troubles generally originate in only one system, but remember that troubles in one system may cause damage to another system or to component engine parts. When a casualty involves more than one system of the engine, trace each system separately and make corrections as necessary. It is obvious that you must know the construction, function, and operation of the various systems as well as the parts of each system for a specific engine before you can satisfactorily locate and remedy troubles.

Even though there are many troubles which may affect the operation of a diesel engine, satisfactory performance depends primarily on the presence of sufficiently high compression pressure and the injection of the right amount of fuel at the proper time. Proper compression depends basically on the pistons, piston rings, and valve gear, while the right amount of fuel obviously depends on the fuel injectors and actuating mechanism. Such troubles as lack of engine power, unusual or erratic operation, and excessive vibration may be caused by either insufficient compression or faulty injector action.

II. TROUBLESHOOTING DIESEL ENGINES

Many of the troubles encountered by an engine operator can be avoided if the prescribed instructions for starting and operating an engine are followed. The lists of troubles which follow cannot be considered complete, and all of these troubles do not necessarily apply to all diesel engines because of differences in design. Specific information on troubleshooting for all the diesel engines used would require more space than is available here.

Even though a successful troubleshooter generally associates a trouble with a particular system or assembly, the troubles we discuss will be according to when they might be encountered, either before or after the engine starts. The troubles are indicative of the system to which they apply. Therefore, further identification is unnecessary.

III. ENGINE FAILS TO START

In general, the troubles which prevent an engine's starting may be grouped under the following headings: (1) the engine can neither be cranked nor barred over, (2) the engine cannot be cranked, but it can be barred over, and (3) the engine can be cranked, but it still fails to start. Figure 1 illustrates various conditions which commonly cause difficulties in cranking, jacking over, or starting the engine.

Engine Cannot Be Cranked
Nor Barred Over

Most prestarting instructions for large engines specify that the crankshaft of an engine should be turned one or more revolutions before starting power is applied. If the crankshaft cannot be turned over, check the turning gear to be sure that it is properly engaged. If the turning gear is properly engaged and the crankshaft still fails to turn over, check to see whether the cylinder test (relief) valves or indicator valves are closed and are holding water or oil in the cylinder. When the turning gear operates properly, and the cylinder test valves are open, but the engine nevertheless cannot be cranked or barred over, the source of the trouble will probably be of a much more serious nature. A piston or other part may be seized or a bearing may be fitting too tightly. Sometimes the difficulty cannot be remedied except by removing a part or an assembly.

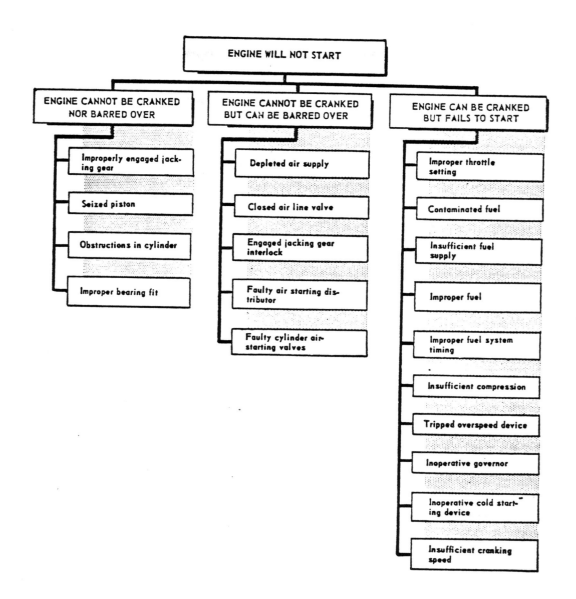

Figure · 1.—Troubles which may prevent a diesel engine's starting.

Some engines have ports through which pistons can be inspected. If inspection reveals that the piston is defective, the assembly must be removed. Figure · 2 illustrates testing for stuck piston rings through the scavenging-air distributor manifold port.

If the condition of an engine without cylinder ports indicates that a piston inspection is required, the whole assembly must be taken out of the cylinder.

Engine bearings have to be carefully fitted or installed according to the manufacturer's instructions. When an engine cannot be jacked over because of an improperly fitted bearing, someone probably failed to follow instructions when the unit was being reassembled.

Engine Cannot Be Cranked But Can Be Barred Over

Most of the troubles that prevent the cranking of an engine, but not serious enough to prevent barring over, can be traced to the starting system although other factors may

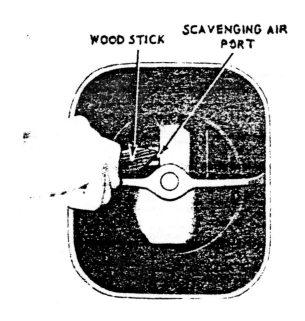

WOOD STICK   SCAVENGING AIR PORT

Figure 2.—Checking the condition of the piston rings.

prevent an engine's cranking. Only troubles related to starting systems are identified in this chapter.

If an engine fails to crank when starting power is applied, first check the turning or jacking gear to be sure that it is disengaged. If this gear is not the source of trouble, then the trouble is probably with the starting system.

IV. AIR STARTING SYSTEM MALFUNCTIONS

Although the design of different air starting systems varies, the function remains the same. In general, such systems must have a source of air such as the compressor or the   air system; a storage tank; air flask(s); an air timing mechanism; and a valve in the engine cylinder to admit the air during starting and to seal the cylinder while the engine is running.

DEFECT IN TIMING MECHANISM.—All air starting systems have a unit designed to admit starting air to the proper cylinder at the proper time. The type of unit as well as its name—timer, distributor, air starting pilot valve, air starting distributor, and air distributor—may vary from one system to another. The types of air timing

mechanisms which may be encountered are the direct mechanical lift, the rotary distributor, and the plunger type distributor valve. The timing mechanism of an air starting system is relatively trouble free except as noted in the following situations.

Direct Mechanical Lift.—The operation of the direct mechanical-lift air timing mechanism involves the use of cams, push rods, and rocker arms, and the mechanism is subject to parts' failures similar to those occurring in corresponding major engine parts. Therefore, the causes of trouble in the actuating gear and the necessary maintenance procedures will be found under information covering similar parts of the major engine systems.

Most troubles are a result of improper adjustment. Generally, this involves the lift of the starting air cam or the timing of the air starting valve. The starting air cam must lift the air starting valve sufficiently to give a proper clearance between the cam and cam valve follower when the engine is running. If proper clearance does not exist between these two parts, hot gases will flow between the valve and the valve seat, causing excessive heating of the parts. Since the starting air cam regulates the opening of the air starting valve, those with adjustable cam lobes should be checked frequently to ensure that the adjusting screws are tight.

The proper values for lift, tappet clearance, and time of valve opening for a direct mechanical lift timing mechanism should be obtained from the manufacturer's technical manual for the particular engine. Make adjustments only as specified.

Rotary Distributor.—The rotary distributor timing mechanism requires a minimum of maintenance, but there may be times when the unit will become inoperative and will have to be disassembled and inspected. Generally, the difficulty is caused by a scored rotor, a broken spring, or improper timing.

Since foreign particles in the air can cause scoring of the rotor, which results in excessive air leakage, the air supply must be kept as clean as possible. Another cause of scoring is lack of lubrication. If the rotor in a hand-oiled system becomes scored because of insufficient lubrication, the equipment could be at fault, or lubrication instructions may not have been followed. In either a hand-oiled or a pressure-lubricated system, check the piping and the passages to see that they are open. When scoring is not too serious, the rotor and body should be lapped together. A thin coat of prussian blue can be used to determine whether the rotor contacts the distributor body.

A broken spring may be the cause of an inoperative timing mechanism if a coil spring is used to maintain the rotor seal. If the spring is broken, replacing the spring is the only way to ensure an effective seal.

An improperly timed rotary distributor will prevent an engine's cranking. Timing should be checked against information given in the instructions for the specific engine.

Plunger Type Distributor Valve.—In a plunger type distributor valve timing mechanism, the valve requires little attention; however, it may stick occasionally and prevent proper functioning of the air starting system. On some engine installations, the pilot air valve of the distributor may not open, while on other installations this valve may not close. The trouble may be caused by dirt and gum deposits, broken return springs, or the lack of lubrication. Deposits and lack of lubrication will cause the unit valve plungers to bind and stick in the guides, while a broken valve return spring prevents the plunger's following the cam profile. A distributor valve that sticks should be disassembled and thoroughly cleaned; any broken springs must be replaced.

FAULTY AIR STARTING VALVES.—Air starting valves admit starting air into the engine cylinder and then seal the cylinder while the engine is running. These valves may be of the pressure-actuated or of the mechanical lift type.

Pressure-Actuated Valves.—In a pressure-actuated valve, the principal trouble encountered is sticking. The valve may stick open for a number of reasons. A gummy or resinous deposit may cause the upper and lower pistons to stick to the cylinders. (This deposit is formed by the oil and condensate which may be

carried into the actuating cylinders and lower cylinders. Oil is necessary in the cylinders to provide lubrication and to act as a seal; however, moisture should be eliminated.) The formation of this resinous deposit can be prevented by draining the system storage tanks and water traps as specified in operating instruction. The deposit on the lower piston may be greater than that in the actuating cylinder because of the heat and combustion gases which add to the formation if the valve remains open. When the upper piston is the source of trouble, sticking can usually be relieved, without removing the valve, by using light oil or diesel fuel and working the valve up and down. When this method is used to relieve a sticking valve, be sure that the valve surfaces are not burned or deformed. If this method does not relieve the sticking condition, the valve will have to be removed, disassembled, and cleaned.

Pressure-actuated starting valves sometimes fail to operate because of broken or weak valve return springs. Replacement is generally the only solution to this condition; however, some valves are constructed with a means of adjusting spring tension. In such valves increasing the spring tension may eliminate the trouble.

Occasionally the actuating pressure of a valve will not release, and the valve will stick open or be sluggish in closing. The cause is usually clogged or restricted air passages. Combustion gases will enter the air passageways, burning the valve surfaces; these burned surfaces usually have to be reconditioned before they will maintain a tight seal. Keeping the air passages open will eliminate extra maintenance work on the valve surfaces.

Mechanical Lift Valves.—The mechanical-lift type air starting valve is subject to leakage which, in general, is caused by the valve's sticking open. Any air starting valve that sticks or leaks creates a condition which makes an engine hard to start. If the leakage in the air starting valve is excessive, the resulting loss in pressure may be sufficient to prevent starting.

Leakage in this type valve can be caused by an over-tightened packing nut. Over-tightening the packing nut is sometimes employed to stop minor leaks around the valve stem when starting pressure is applied, but it may prevent seating of the air valve. As in the pressure-actuated valve, return spring tension may be insufficient to return the valve to the valve seat after admitting the air charge. If this occurs, gases from the cylinder will leak into the valve while the engine is running.

Obstructions such as particles of carbon between the valve and valve seat will hold the valve open, permitting combustion gases to pass. A valve stem bent by careless handling during installation also may prevent a valve's closing properly.

If a valve hangs open for any of these reasons, hot combustion gases will leak past the valve and valve seat. The gases burn the valve and seat and may result in a leak between these two surfaces even though the original causes of the stocking are eliminated.

A leaking valve should be completely disassembled and inspected. It is subject to a resinous deposit similar to that found in a pressure-actuated air valve. A specified cleaning compound should be used for the removal of the deposit. Be sure the valve stem is not bent. Check the valve and valve seat surfaces carefully. Scoring or discoloration should be eliminated by lapping with a fine lapping compound. Jewelers' rouge or talcum powder with fuel oil may be used for lapping.

From the preceding discussion, you can readily see that the air starting system may be the source of many troubles that will prevent an engine's cranking even though it can be barred over. A few of the troubles can be avoided if prestarting and starting instructions are followed. One such instruction, sometimes overlooked, is that of opening the valve in the air line. Obviously, with this valve closed the engine will not crank. Recheck the instructions for such an oversight as a closed valve, an empty air storage receiver, or an engaged jacking gear before starting any disassembly.

V. ELECTRIC START MALFUNCTIONS

Electric starting system malfunctions fall into the following categories:

1. Nothing happens when the starter switch is closed.

2. Starter motor runs but does not engage the engine.

3. Starter motor engages but cannot turn the engine.

The first situation is the result of an electrical system failure. The failure could be an open circuit caused by broken connections or burned out components. Circuit continuity should be tested to ensure that the relay closes and that the battery provides sufficient voltage and current to the starter circuit. If the circuit is complete, there may be resistance through faulty battery connections. Considerable current is needed to operate the solenoid and starter motor.

If the starter runs free of engagement, it will produce a distinctive hum or whine. The lack of engagement is usually caused by dirt or corrosion which prevents proper operation of the solenoid or Bendix gears.

If the starter motor engages the flywheel ring gear but is either not able to turn the engine or cannot turn it quickly enough to obtain starting speed, the cause may be lack of battery power, or more likely, a mechanical problem. If the engine can be barred over, there is excessive friction in the meshing of the starter pinion and the ring gear. Either the teeth are deformed, or the starter pinion is out of alignment. Either case would have been preceded by noise the last time the starter was used. A major repair may be necessary.

Engine Cranks But
Fails To Start

Even when the starting equipment is in an operating condition, an engine may fail to start. A majority of the possible troubles which prevent an engine's starting are associated with fuel and the fuel system. However, parts or assemblies which are defective or inoperative may be the source of some trouble. Failure to follow instructions may be the cause of an engine failing to start. The corrective action is obvious for such items as leaving the fuel throttle in the OFF position and leaving the cylinder indicator valves open. If an engine fails to start, follow prescribed starting instructions and recheck the procedure.

FOREIGN MATTER IN THE FUEL OIL SYSTEM.—In the operation of an internal-combustion engine, cleanliness is of paramount importance. This is especially true in the handling and care of diesel fuel oil. Impurities are the prime source of fuel pump and injection system troubles. Sediment and water cause wear, gumming, corrosion, and rust in a fuel system. Even though fuel oil is generally delivered clean from the refinery, handling and transferring increase the chances of fuel oil's becoming contaminated.

Corrosion frequently leads to replacement or at least to repair of the part. Steps should be taken continually to prevent the accumulation of water in a fuel system, not only to eliminate the cause of corrosion but also to ensure proper combustion in the cylinders. All fuel should be centrifuged, and the fuel filter cases should be drained periodically to prevent excessive collection of water.

Water in fuel is injurious to the entire fuel system and will cause irreparable damage in a short time. It not only corrodes the fuel injection pump, where close clearances must be maintained, but also corrodes and erodes the injection nozzles. The slightest corrosion can cause a fuel injection pump to bind and seize and, if not corrected, will lead to excessive leakage. Water will cause the orifices of injection nozzles to erode until they will not spray the fuel properly, thus preventing proper atomization. When this occurs, incomplete combustion and engine knocks result.

Air in the fuel system is another possible trouble which may prevent an engine's starting. Even if starting is possible, air in the fuel system will cause the engine to miss and knock, and perhaps to stall.

When an engine fails to operate, stalls, misfires, or knocks, there may be air in the high-pressure pumps and lines. In many systems, the expansion and compression of such air may take place without the injection valves' opening. If this occurs, the pump is AIRBOUND. You can determine whether air exists in a fuel system by bleeding a small amount of fuel from the top of the fuel filter; if the fuel appears quite cloudy, there are probably small bubbles of air in the fuel.

INSUFFICIENT FUEL SUPPLY.—An insufficient fuel supply may result from any one of a number of defective or inoperative parts in the system. Such items as a closed inlet valve in the fuel piping or an empty supply tank are more apt to be the fault of the operator than of the equipment. But an empty tank may be caused by leakage, either in the lines or in the tank.

Leakage.—Leakage in the low-pressure lines of a fuel system can usually be traced to cracks in the piping; usually these cracks occur on threaded pipe joints at the root of the threads. Such breakage is caused by the inability of the nipples and pipe joints to withstand shock, vibration, and strains resulting from the relative motion between smaller pipes and the equipment to which they are attached.

Metal fatigue can also be a cause of breakage; each system should have a systematic inspection of the installation of fittings and piping to determine whether all parts are satisfactorily supported and sufficiently strong. In some instances, nipples may be connected to relatively heavy parts, such as valves and strainers, which are free to vibrate. Since vibration contributes materially to the fatigue of nipples, rigid bracing should be installed. When practicable, bracing should be secured to the unit itself, instead of to the hull or other equipment.

Leakage in the high-pressure lines of a fuel system also results from breakage. The breakage usually occurs on either of the two end fittings of a line and is caused by lack of proper supports or by excessive nozzle opening pressure. Supports are usually supplied with an engine and should not be discarded. Excessive opening pressure of a nozzle—generally due to improper spring adjustment or to clogged nozzle orifices—may rupture the high-pressure fuel lines. A faulty nozzle generally requires removal, inspection, and repair plus the use of a nozzle tester.

Leakage from fuel lines may be due also to improper replacements or repairs. When a replacement is necessary, always use a line of the same length and diameter as the one removed. Varying the length and diameter of a high-pressure fuel line will change the injection characteristics of the injection nozzle.

In an emergency, high-pressure fuel lines can usually be satisfactorily repaired by silver soldering a new fitting to the line. After making a silver solder repair, test the line for leaks and be certain no restrictions exist.

Most leakage trouble occurs in the fuel lines, but leaks may occasionally develop in the fuel tank. These leaks must be eliminated immediately, because of potential fire hazard.

The principal causes of fuel tank leakage are improper welds and metal fatigue. Metal fatigue is usually the result of inadequate support at the source of trouble; excessive stresses develop in the tank, and cracks result.

Clogged Fuel Filters.—Another factor that can limit the fuel supply to such an extent that an engine will not start is the clogged fuel filters. As soon as it is known that clogging exists, the filter elements should be replaced. Definite rules for such replacement cannot be established for all engines. Instructions generally state that elements will not be used longer than a specified time, and there are reasons that an element may not function properly even for the specified interval.

Filter elements may become clogged because of dirty fuel, too small filter capacity, failure to drain the filter sump, and failure to use the primary strainer. Usually, clogging is indicated by such symptoms as stoppage of fuel flow, increase in pressure drop across the filter, increase in pressure upstream of the filter, or excessive accumulation of dirt on the element (observed when the filter is removed for inspection). Symptoms of clogged filters vary in different installations, and each installation should be studied for external symptoms, such as abnormal instrument indications and engine operation. If external indications are not apparent, visual inspection of the element will be necessary, especially if it is known or suspected that dirty fuel is being used.

Fuel filter capacity should at least equal fuel supply pump capacity. A filter with a small capacity clogs more rapidly than a larger one, because the space available for dirt accumulation is more limited. There are two standardized sizes of fuel filter elements—large and small. The small element is the same diameter as the large but is only one-half as long. This construction permits substitution of two small elements for one large element.

The interval of time between element changes can be increased by making use of the drain cocks on a filter sump; removal of dirt through the drain cock will make room for more dirt to collect.

If new filter elements are not available for replacement and the engine must be operated, you can wash some types of totally clogged elements and get limited additional service. This procedure is for emergencies only. An engine must never be operated unless all the fuel is filtered, therefore a "washed filter" is better than none at all.

Fuel must never flow from the supply tanks to the nozzles without passing through all stages of filtration. Strainers, as the primary stage in the fuel filtration system, must be kept in good condition if sufficient fuel is to flow in the system. Most strainers are equipped with a blade mechanism which is designed to be turned by hand. If the scraper element cannot be turned readily by hand, the strainer should be disassembled and cleaned. This minor preventive maintenance will prevent breakage of the scraping mechanism.

Transfer Pumps.—If the supply of fuel oil to the system is to be maintained in an even and uninterrupted flow, the fuel transfer pumps must be functioning properly. These pumps may become inoperative or defective to the point that they fail to discharge sufficient fuel for engine starting. Generally, when a pump fails to operate, some parts have to be replaced or reconditioned. For some types of pump, it is customary to replace the entire unit. However, for worn packing or seals, satisfactory repairs may be made. If plunger-type pumps fail to operate because the valves have become dirty, submerge and clean the pump in a bath of diesel oil.

Repairs of fuel transfer pumps should be made in accordance with maintenance manuals supplied by the individual pump manufacturers.

VI. MALFUNCTIONING OF THE INJECTION SYSTEM.—The fuel injection system is the most intricate of the systems in a diesel engine, and the troubles which may occur depend on the system in use. Since an injection system functions to deliver fuel to the cylinder at a high pressure, at the proper time, in the proper quantities, and properly atomized, it is evident that special care and precautions must be taken in making adjustments and repairs.

High-Pressure Pump.—If a high-pressure pump in a fuel injection system becomes inoperative, an engine may fail to start. Information on the troubles which make a pump inoperative, and the information necessary for overcoming such troubles, is more than can be given in the space available here.

Timing.—Regardless of the installation or the type of fuel injection system used, maximum energy obtainable from fuel cannot be gained if the timing of the injection system is incorrect. Early or late injection timing may prevent an engine's starting. If the engine does start, it will not perform satisfactorily. Operation will be uneven and vibration will be greater than usual.

If fuel enters a cylinder too early, detonation generally results, causing the gas pressure to rise too rapidly before the piston reaches top dead center. This in turn causes a loss of power and high combustion pressures. Low exhaust temperatures may be an indication that fuel injection is too early.

When fuel is injected too late in the engine cycle, overheating, lowered firing pressure, smoky exhaust, high exhaust temperatures, or loss of power may occur.

Correction of an improperly timed injection system should be accomplished by following the instructions given in the appropriate manufacturer's technical manual.

INSUFFICIENT COMPRESSION.—Proper compression pressures are essential if a diesel engine is to operate satisfactorily. Insufficient compression may be the reason that an engine fails to start. If low pressure is suspected as the reason, compression should be checked with the appropriate instrument. If the test indicates pressures below standard, disassembly is required for complete inspection and correction.

INOPERATIVE ENGINE GOVERNOR.—There are many troubles which may render a governor inoperative, but those encountered in starting an engine are generally caused by bound control linkage or, if the governor is hydraulic, by low oil level. Whether the governor is mechanical or hydraulic, binding of linkage is generally due to distorted, misaligned, defective, or dirty parts. If binding is suspected, linkage and governor parts should be moved and checked by hand. Any undue stiffness or sluggishness in the movement of the linkage should be eliminated.

Low oil level in hydraulic governors may be due to leakage of oil from the governor, or to failure to maintain the proper oil level. Leakage of oil from a governor can generally be traced to a faulty oil seal on the drive shaft or power piston rod, or to a poor gasket seal between parts of the governor case.

The condition of oil seals should be checked if oil must be added too frequently to governors with independent oil supplies. Dependent on the point of leakage, oil seal leakage may or may not be visible on external surfaces. There will be no external sign if leakage occurs through the seal around the drive shaft, while leakage through the seal around the power piston will be visible.

Oil seals must be kept clean and pliable; therefore, the seals must be properly stored so that they do not become dry and brittle, or dirty. The repair of leaky oil seals requires a replacement. Some of the leakage troubles can be prevented if proper installation and storage instructions for oil seals are followed.

INOPERATIVE OVERSPEED SAFETY DEVICES.—Overspeed safety devices are designed to shut off fuel or air in the event engine speed becomes excessive. It is imperative that these devices be maintained in operable condition at all times. Inoperative overspeed devices may cause an engine not to start. They may be inoperative because of improper adjustment, faulty linkage, a broken spring, or the overspeed device may have been accidentally tripped during the attempt to start the engine. The overspeed device must always be put in an operative condition before the engine is operated.

If the overspeed device fails to operate when the engine overspeeds, the engine may be secured by manually cutting off the fuel oil or the air supply to the engine. Most engines are equipped with special devices or valves to cut off the air or fuel in an emergency.

INSUFFICIENT CRANKING SPEED.—If the engine cranks slowly, the necessary compression temperature cannot be reached. Low starting air pressure may be the source of such trouble.

Slow cranking speed may also be the result of an increase in the viscosity of the lubricating oil. This trouble is encountered during periods when the air temperature is lower than usual. The oil specified for use during normal operation and temperature is not generally suitable for cold climate operation.

VII. IRREGULAR ENGINE OPERATION

The engine operator must constantly be alert to detect any symptoms which might indicate the existence of trouble. Forewarning is often given in the form of sudden or abnormal changes in the supply, the temperature, or the pressure of the lubricating oil or of the cooling water. Color and temperature of exhaust afford warning of abnormal conditions and should be checked frequently. Fuel, oil, and water leaks are an indication of possible troubles. Keep the engine clean to make such leaks easier to spot.

An operator soon becomes accustomed to the "normal" sounds and vibrations of a properly operating engine. An abnormal or unexpected change in the pitch or tone of an engine's noise, or a change in the magnitude or frequency of a vibration, warns the alert

operator that all is not well. The occurrence of a new sound such as a knock, a drop in the fuel injection pressure, or a misfiring cylinder are other trouble warnings for which an operator should be constantly alert during engine operation.

The following discussion on possible troubles, their causes, and the corrective action necessary, is general rather than specific. The information is based on instructions for some of the engines used, and it is typical of most, though not all, models of diesel engines for use. A few troubles listed may apply to only one model. For specific information on any particular engine, consult the manufacturer's technical manual.

Engine Stalls Frequently Or Stops Suddenly

Several of the troubles which may cause an engine to stall or stop were discussed earlier under starting troubles. Such troubles as air in the fuel system, clogged fuel filters, unsatisfactory operation of fuel injection equipment, and incorrect governor action not only cause starting failures or stalling but also may cause other troubles as well. For example, clogged fuel oil filters and strainers may lead to loss of power, to misfires or erratic firing, or to low fuel oil pressure. Unfortunately, a single engine trouble does not always manifest itself as a single difficulty but may be the cause of several major difficulties.

Factors which may cause an engine to stall include the following: misfiring, low cooling water temperature, improper application of load, improper timing, obstruction in the combustion space or in the exhaust system, insufficient intake air, piston seizure, and defective auxiliary drive mechanisms.

MISFIRING.—When an engine misfires or fires erratically, or when one cylinder misfires regularly, the possible troubles can usually be associated with the fuel or fuel system, worn parts, or the air cleaner or silencer. In determining what causes a cylinder to misfire, you should follow prescribed procedures given in the appropriate technical manual. Procedures will vary among engines because of differences in the design of parts and equipment.

Many of the troubles resulting from fuel contamination require overhaul and repair. However, a cylinder may misfire regularly in some systems because of the fuel pump cut-out mechanism. Some fuel pumps are equipped with this type of mechanism so that fuel supply can be cut off from a cylinder to measure compression pressures. You should check first for an engaged cut-out mechanism (if installed) when a cylinder is misfiring and disengage it during normal engine operation.

Loss Of Compression.—A cylinder may misfire due to loss of compression which may be caused by a leaking cylinder head gasket, by leaking or sticking cylinder valves, by worn pistons, liners, or rings, or by a cracked cylinder head or block. If loss of compression pressure causes an engine to misfire, a check of the compression pressure of each cylinder should be made. Some indicators are designed to measure compression as well as firing pressure while the engine is running at full speed. Others are designed to check only the compression pressures with the engine running at a relatively slow speed. Figure 3 illustrates the application of some different types of pressure indicators.

After an indicator is installed, operate the engine at the specified rpm and record the cylinder compression pressure. Follow this procedure on each cylinder in turn. The pressure in any one cylinder should not be lower than the specified psi, nor should the pressure for any one cylinder be excessively lower than the pressures in the other cylinders. The maximum pressure variation permitted between cylinders is given on engine data sheets or in the manufacturer's technical manual. A compression leak is indicated when the pressure in one cylinder is considerably lower than that in the other cylinders.

A test indicating a compression leak means some disassembly, inspection, and repair. The valve seats and cylinder head gaskets must be checked for leaks and the valve stems must be inspected for sticking. A cylinder head or block may be cracked. If these parts are not the source of trouble, compression is probably leaking past

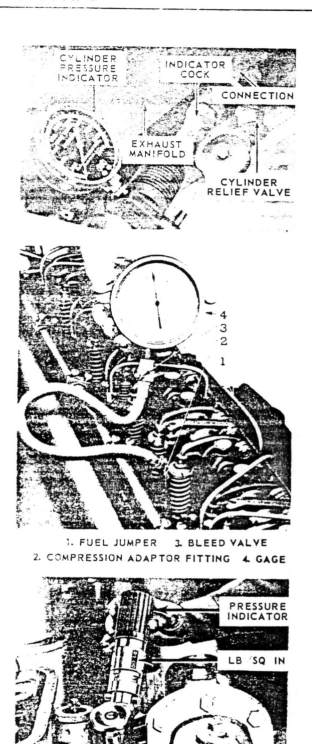

1. FUEL JUMPER   3. BLEED VALVE
2. COMPRESSION ADAPTOR FITTING 4. GAGE

Figure   3.—Engine cylinder pressure indicator applications.

the piston because of insufficient sealing of the piston rings.

Clogged Air Cleaners And Silencers.—Sometimes the reason for an engine's firing erratically or misfiring is clogged air cleaners and silencers. Air cleaners must be cleaned at specified intervals, as recommended in the engine manufacturer's technical manuals. A clogged cleaner reduces the intake air, thereby affecting the operation of the engine. Clogged air cleaners may cause not only misfiring or erratic firing but also such difficulties as hard starting, loss of power, engine smoke, and overheating.

When a volatile solvent is used for cleaning an air cleaner element, it is of extreme importance that the cleaner be dry before it is reinstalled on the engine. Volatile solvents are excellent cleaning agents but, if permitted to remain in the filter, may be the cause of engine overspeeding or a serious explosion.

Oil bath type air cleaners and filters are the source of very little trouble if serviced properly. Cleaning directions are generally given on the cleaner housing. The frequency of cleaning is usually based on a specified number of operating hours, but more frequent cleanings may be necessary where unfavorable conditions exist.

When filling an oil bath type cleaner, follow the manufacturer's filling instructions. Most air cleaners of this type have a FULL mark on the oil reservoir. Filling beyond this mark does not increase the efficiency of the unit and may lead to serious trouble. When the oil bath is too full, the intake air may draw oil into the cylinders. This excess oil-air mixture, over which there is no control, may cause an engine to "run away," resulting in serious damage.

LOW COOLING WATER TEMPERATURE.—If an engine is to operate properly, the cooling water temperature must be maintained within specified temperature limits. When cooling water temperature becomes lower than recommended for a diesel engine, ignition lag is increased, causing detonation, which results in "rough" operation and may cause an engine to stall.

The thermostatic valves that control cooling water temperature operate with a minimum of

trouble. Cooling water temperatures above or below the value specified in the technical manual sometimes indicate that the thermostat is inoperative. However, high or low cooling water temperature does not always indicate thermostat trouble. The engine load may be insufficient to maintain proper cooling water temperatures, or the temperature gage may be inaccurate or inoperative. Check these items before removing a thermostatic control unit.

When a thermostat is suspected of faulty operation, it must be removed from the engine and tested.

A thermostat may be checked as follows:

1. A container which does not block or distort vision is needed. Fill the container, preferably a glass beaker, with water.

2. Heat the water to the temperature at which the thermostat is supposed to start opening. This temperature is usually specified in the appropriate technical manual. Use an accurate thermometer to keep a check on the water temperature. A hot plate or a burner may be used as a source of heat. Stir the water frequently to ensure uniform distribution of the heat.

3. Suspend the thermostat in such a manner that operation of the bellows will not be restricted. A wire or string will serve as a satisfactory means of suspension.

4. Immerse the thermostat and observe its action. Check the thermometer readings carefully to see whether the thermostat begins to open at the recommended temperature. (The thermostat and thermometer must NOT touch the container.)

5. Increase the temperature of the water until the specified FULL OPEN temperature is reached. The immersed thermostatic valve should be fully open at this temperature.

The thermostat should be replaced if, when it is tested, there is no movement, or if there is a divergence of more than a specified number of degrees between the temperature at which the thermostat begins to open, or opens fully, and the actuating temperatures specified in the manufacturer's technical manual.

The Fulton-Sylphon automatic temperature regulator is relatively trouble-free. The unit controls temperatures by positioning a valve to bypass some water around the cooler. This system provides for a full flow of the water although only a portion may be cooled. In other words, the full volume of cooling water is circulated at the proper velocity, which eliminates the possibility of the formation of steam pockets in the system.

Generally, when the automatic temperature regulator fails to maintain cooling water at the proper temperature, improper adjustment is indicated. However, the element of the valve may be leaking or some part of the valve may be defective. Failure to follow the proper adjustment procedure is the only cause for improper adjustment of an automatic temperature regulator. Check and follow the proper procedure in the manufacturer's technical manual issued for the specific equipment.

The adjustment consists of changing the tension of the spring (which opposes the action of the thermostatic bellows) with a special tool which is used to turn the adjusting stem knob or wheel. Increasing the spring tension raises the temperature range of the regulator, and decreasing it lowers the temperature range.

When a new valve of this type is placed in service, a number of steps must be taken to ensure that the valve stem length is proper and that all scale pointers make accurate indications. All adjustments should be made in accordance with the valve manufacturer's technical manual.

OBSTRUCTION IN THE COMBUSTION SPACE.—Such items as broken valve heads and valve stem locks, or keepers, which come loose because of a broken valve spring, may cause an engine to come to an abrupt stop. If an engine continues to run when such obstructions are in the combustion chamber, the piston, liner, head, and injection nozzle will be severely damaged.

OBSTRUCTION IN THE EXHAUST SYSTEM.—This type of trouble is seldom encountered if proper installation and maintenance procedures are followed. When a part of an engine exhaust system is restricted, an increase in the exhaust back pressure will result. This may cause high exhaust temperatures, loss of power, or even stalling. An obstruction which causes excessive back pressure in an exhaust system is generally associated with the silencer or muffler.

The manifolds of an exhaust system are relatively trouble-free if related equipment is designed and installed properly. Improper design or installation may result in water's backing up into the exhaust manifold. In some installations, silencer design may be the cause of water's flowing into the engine. The source of water which may enter an engine must be found and eliminated. This may require replacing some parts of the exhaust system with components of an improved design, or may require relocating such items as the silencer and piping.

Inspect exhaust manifolds for water or symptoms of water. Accumulation of salt or scale in the manifold usually indicates that water has been entering from the silencer. Turbochargers on some engines have been known to seize because of salt water's entering the exhaust gas turbine from the silencer. Entry of water into an engine may be detected also by the presence of corrosion or of salt deposits on the engine exhaust valves. If inspection reveals signs of water in an engine or in the exhaust manifold, steps should be taken immediately to correct the trouble. Check the unit for proper installation. Wet-type silencers must be installed with the proper sizes of piping. If the inlet water piping is too large, an excess of water may be injected into the silencer. If a silencer has no continuous drain and the engine is at a lower level than the exhaust outlet, water may back up into the engine.

Dry-type silencers may become clogged with an excessive accumulation of oil or soot. When this occurs, exhaust back pressure increases, causing troubles such as high exhaust temperatures, loss of power, or possibly stalling. A dry-type silencer clogged with oil or soot is also subject to fire. Clogging can usually be detected by fire, soot, or sparks which may come from the exhaust stack. An excessive accumulation of oil or soot in a dry-type silencer may be due to a number of factors, such as failure to drain the silencer, poor condition of the engine, or improper engine operating conditions.

Silencers should be cleaned of oil and soot accumulations at necessary intervals. Even though recommended cleaning periods may be specified, conditions of operation may require more frequent inspections and cleaning. For example, an accumulation of soot and oil is more likely to occur during periods of prolonged idling than when the engine is operating under a normal load. Idling periods should be held to a minimum.

INSUFFICIENT INTAKE AIR.—Insufficient intake air, which may cause an engine to stall or stop, may be due to blower failure or to a clogged air silencer or air filter. Even though all other engine parts function perfectly, efficient engine operation is impossible if the air intake system fails to supply a sufficient quantity of air for complete combustion of the fuel.

Troubles that may prevent a centrifugal blower's performing its function generally involve damage to the rotor shaft, thrust bearings, turbine blading, nozzle ring, or blower impeller. Damage to the rotor shaft and thrust bearings usually occurs as a result of insufficient lubrication, an unbalanced rotor, or operation with excessive exhaust temperature.

Centrifugal blower lubrication difficulties may be caused by failure of the oil pump to prime, low lube oil level, clogged oil passages or oil filter, or a defect in the relief valve which is designed to maintain proper lube oil pressure.

If an unbalanced rotor is the cause of shaft or bearing trouble, there will be excessive vibration. Unbalance may be caused by a damaged turbine wheel blading, or by a damaged blower impeller.

Operating a blower when the exhaust temperature is above the specified maximum safe temperature generally causes severe damage to turbocharger bearings and other parts. Every effort should be made to find and eliminate causes of excessive exhaust temperature before the turbocharger is damaged.

Turbine blading damage in a centrifugal-type blower may be caused by operating with an excessive exhaust temperature, operating at excessive speeds, bearing failures, failure to drain the turbine casing, the entrance of foreign bodies, or turbine blades which break loose.

Damage to an impeller of a centrifugal blower may result from thrust or shaft bearing failure, entrance of foreign bodies, or loosening of the impeller on the shaft.

Since blowers are high-speed units and operate with a very small clearance between parts, minor damage to a part might result in extensive blower damage and failure.

Although there is considerable difference in principle and construction of the positive-displacement blower (Roots) and the axial-flow positive-displacement blower (Hamilton-Whitfield), the problems of operation and maintenance are similar.

Some of the troubles encountered in a positive-displacement type blower are similar to those already mentioned in our discussion of the centrifugal-type blowers. However, the source of some troubles may be different because of construction differences.

Positive-displacement type blowers are equipped with a set of gears to drive and synchronize the rotation of the rotors. Many of these blowers are driven by a serrated shaft. Regardless of construction differences, the basic problem in both types of blowers is to maintain the necessary small clearances. If these clearances are not maintained, the rotors and the case will be damaged, and the blower will fail to perform its function.

Worn gears are one source of trouble in positive-displacement type blowers. A certain amount of gear wear is expected, but damage resulting from excessively worn gears indicates improper maintenance procedures. During inspections, the values of backlash should be recorded in the material history. This record can be used to establish the rate of increase in wear, to estimate the life of the gears, and to determine when it will be necessary to replace the gears.

Scored rotor lobes and casing may cause blower failure. Scoring of blower parts may be caused by worn gears, improper timing, bearing failure, improper end clearance, or by foreign matter. Any of these troubles may be serious enough to cause contact of the rotors and extensive damage to the blower.

Timing of blower rotors not only involves gear backlash but also the clearances between

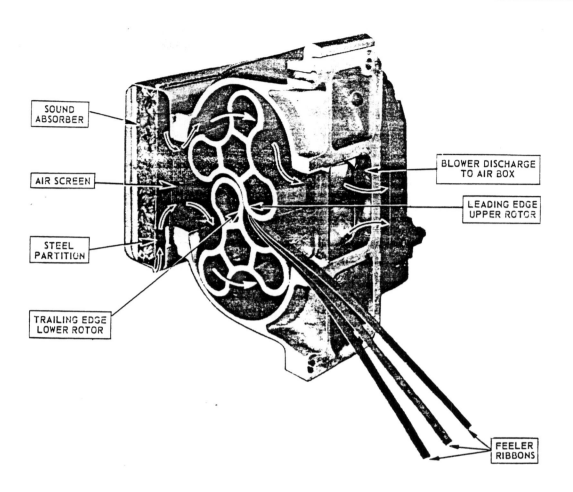

Figure 4.—Checking clearances of positive-displacement blower lobes.

leading and trailing edges of the rotor lobes and between rotor lobes and casing. Clearance between these parts can be measured with thickness gages, as illustrated in figure 4. If clearances are incorrect, check the backlash of the drive gear first. If the backlash is excessive, the gears must be replaced. Then the rotors must be retimed according to the method outlined in the appropriate manufacturer's technical manual.

Failure of serrated blower shafts may be the result of failure to inspect the parts or of improper replacement of parts. When inspecting serrated shafts, be sure that they fit snugly and that wear is not excessive. When serrations of either the shaft or hub have failed for any reason, both parts must be replaced.

PISTON SEIZURE.—Piston seizure may be the cause of an engine's stopping suddenly. The piston becomes galled and scuffed. When this occurs, the piston may possibly break or extensive damage may be done to other major engine parts. The principal causes of piston seizure are insufficient clearance, excessive temperatures, or inadequate lubrication.

DEFECTIVE AUXILIARY DRIVE MECHANISMS.—Defects in auxiliary drive mechanisms may cause an engine to stop suddenly. Since most troubles in gear trains or chain drives require some disassembly, we shall limit our discussion to only the causes of such troubles.

Gear failure is the principal trouble encountered in gear trains. Engine failure and extensive damage can occur because of a broken or chipped gear. If you hear a metallic clicking noise in the vicinity of a gear housing, it is almost a certain indication that a gear tooth has broken.

Gears are most likely to fail because of improper lubrication, corrosion, misalignment, torsional vibration, excessive backlash, wiped bearings and bushings, metal obstructions, or improper manufacturing procedures.

Gear shafts, bushings and bearings, and gear teeth must be checked during periodic inspections for scoring, wear, and pitting. All oil passages, jets, and sprays should be cleaned to ensure proper oil flow. All gear-locking devices must fit tightly to prevent longitudinal gear movement.

Chains are used in some engines for camshaft and auxiliary drives; in others, they are used to drive certain auxiliary rotating parts. Troubles encountered in chain drives usuall. wear or breakage. Troubles of this be caused by improper tension lubrication, sheared cotter misalignment.

Figure 5 is a summary of the troubles which may cause an engine t frequently or stop suddenly. Some doub. exist as to the difference between stalling stopping. In reality, there is none unless associate certain troubles with each. In general, troubles which cause FREQUENT STALLING are those which can be eliminated with minor adjustments or maintenance. If such troubles are not eliminated, it is quite possible that the engine can be started, only to stall again. Failure to eliminate some of the troubles which cause frequent stalling may lead to troubles with cause SUDDEN STOPPING.

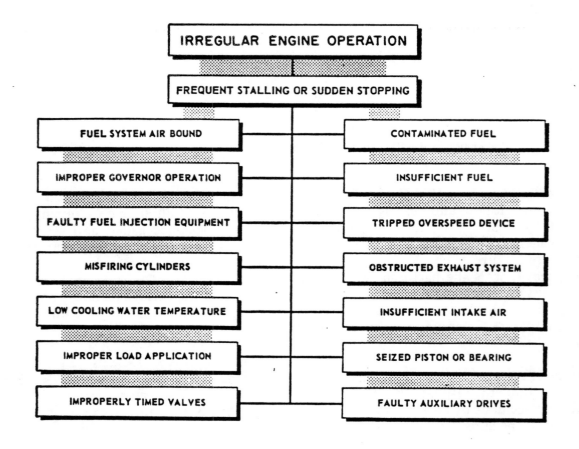

Figure 5.—Possible troubles which may cause an engine to stall frequently or to stop suddenly.

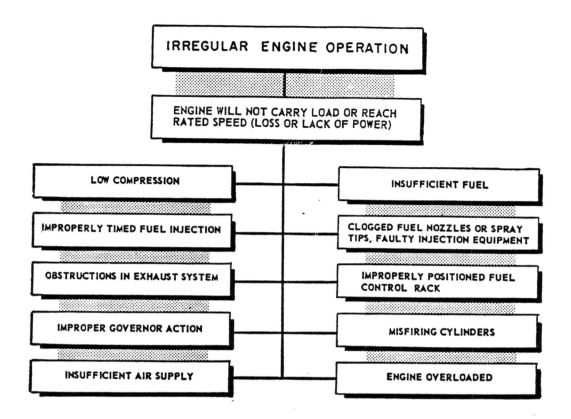

Figure 6.—Possible causes of insufficient power in an engine.

Engine Will Not Carry Load

Many of the troubles which can lead to loss of power in an engine may also cause the engine to stop and stall suddenly, or may even prevent its starting. Compare the list of some of the troubles that may cause a power loss in the engine in figure 6 with those in figures 1 and 5. Such items as insufficient air, insufficient fuel, and faulty operation of the governor appear on all three charts. Many of the troubles listed are closely related, and the elimination of one may eliminate others.

The operator of an internal-combustion engine may be confronted with additional major difficulties, such as those indicated in figure 7. Here, again, you can see that many of these possible troubles are similar to those already discussed in connection with starting failures and with engine stalling and stopping. The discussion which follows covers only those troubles not previously considered.

Engine Overspeeds

When an engine overspeeds, the trouble can usually be associated with either the governor mechanism or the fuel control linkage, as previously discussed. When information on a specific fuel system or speed control system is required, check the manufacturer's technical manual and the special technical manuals for the particular equipment. These special manuals are available for the most widely used models of hydraulic governors and overspeed trips, and they contain specific details on testing, adjusting, and repairing.

Engine Hunts or Will Not Secure

Some troubles which may cause an engine to hunt are similar to those which may cause an engine to resist securing efforts. Generally, these two forms of irregular engine operation are

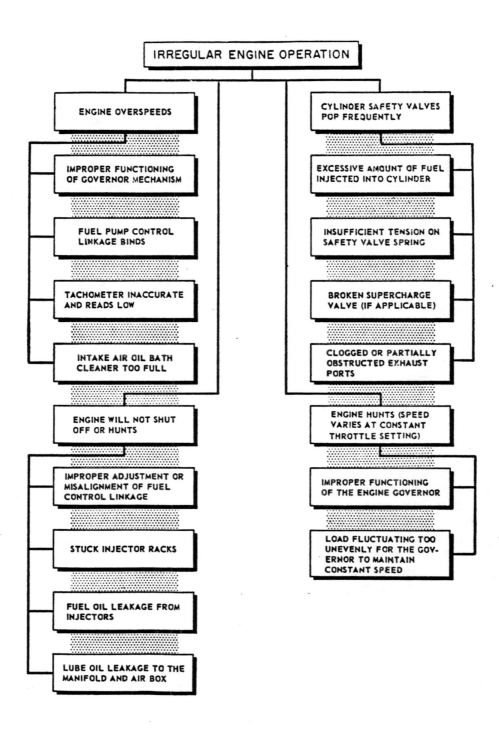

Figure 7.—Additional causes of irregular engine operation.

caused by troubles originating in the fuel system and speed control system.

SPEED CONTROL SYSTEM.—The speed control system of an internal-combustion engine includes those parts designed to maintain the engine speed at some exact value, or between desired limits, regardless of changes in load on the engine. Governors are provided to regulate fuel injection so that the speed of the engine can be controlled as the load is applied. The governor also acts to prevent overspeeding as in rough seas when the load might be suddenly reduced when the propellers leave the water.

If certain parts of the fuel system or governor fail to function properly, the engine may hunt—that is, vary at a constant throttle setting—or it may be difficult to stop the engine.

FUEL CONTROL RACKS.—Fuel control racks that have become sticky or jammed may cause governing difficulties. If the control rack of a fuel system is not functioning properly, the engine speed may decrease as the load is removed or the engine may hunt continuously, or it may hunt only when the load is changed. A sticky or jammed control rack may prevent an engine's responding to changes in throttle setting and may even prevent securing. Any such condition could be serious in an emergency situation. Your job is to make every effort possible to prevent the occurrence of such conditions.

You can check for a sticky rack by securing the engine, disconnecting the linkage to the governor, and then attempting to move the rack by hand. There should be no apparent resistance to the motion of the rack if the return springs and linkage are disconnected. A stuck control rack may be caused by the plunger's sticking in the pump barrel; dirt in the rack mechanism; damage to the rack, sleeve, or gear; or improper assembly of the injector pump.

The cause of sticking or jamming must be determined and damaged parts must be replaced. If sticking is due to dirt, a thorough cleaning of all parts will probably correct the trouble. Errors in assembly can be avoided by carefully studying the assembly drawings and instructions.

LEAKAGE OF FUEL OIL.—Leakage of fuel oil from the injectors may cause an engine to continue to operate when you attempt to shut it down. Regardless of the type of fuel system, the results of internal leakage from injection equipment are, in general, somewhat the same. Injector leakage will cause unsatisfactory engine operation because of the excessive amount of fuel entering the cylinder. Leakage may also cause detonation, crankcase dilution, smoky exhaust, loss of power, and excessive carbon formation on spray tips of nozzles and other surfaces of the combustion chamber.

ACCUMULATION OF LUBE OIL.—Another trouble which may prevent stopping an engine is accumulation of lube oil in the intake air passages—manifold or air box. Such an accumulation creates an extremely dangerous condition. Excess oil can be detected by removing inspection plates on covers and examining the air box and manifold. If oil is discovered, it should be removed and the necessary corrective maintenance should be performed. If oil is drawn suddenly in large quantities from the manifold or air box into the cylinder of the engine and burns, the engine may run away. The engine governor has no control over the sudden increase of speed that occurs.

An air box or air manifold explosion is also a possibility if excess oil is allowed to accumulate. Some engine manufacturers have provided safety devices to reduce the hazards of such explosions.

Excess oil in the air box or manifold of an engine also increases the tendency toward carbon formation on liner ports, cylinder valves, and other parts of the combustion chamber.

The causes of excessive lube oil accumulation in the air box or manifold will vary depending on the specific engine. Generally, the accumulation is due to an obstruction in either the air box or separator drains.

In an effort to reduce the possibility of crankcase explosions and runaways, some engine manufacturers have designed a means to ventilate the crankcase. In some engines, ventilation is accomplished by a passage between the crankcase and the intake side of the blower. In other engines, an oil separator or air maze is provided in the passage between the crankcase and blower intake.

In either type of installation, stoppage of the drains will cause an excessive accumulation of oil. It is essential that drain passages be kept open by being properly cleaned whenever necessary.

Oil may enter the air box or manifold from sources other than crankcase vapors. A defective blower oil seal, a carryover from an oil type air cleaner, or defective oil piping may be the source of trouble.

Another possible source may be an excessively high oil level in the crankcase. Under this condition, an oil fog is created in some engines by moving the parts. An oil fog may be caused also by excessive clearance in the connecting rod and main journal bearings. In some types of crankcase ventilating systems, the oil fog will be drawn into the blower. When this occurs, an abnormal amount of oil may accumulate in the air box. Removal of the oil will not remove the trouble. The cause of the accumulation must be determined and the necessary repair must be accomplished.

If a blower oil seal is defective, replacement is the only satisfactory method of correction. When installing new seals, be sure the shafts are not scored and the bearings are in satisfactory condition. Special precautions must be taken during installation to avoid damaging oil seals. Damage to an oil seal during installation is usually not discovered until the blower has been reinstalled and the engine has been put into operation. Be sure an oil seal gets the necessary lubrication. The oil not only lubricates the seal, reducing friction, but also carries away any heat that is generated. New oil seals are generally soaked in clean, light lube oil before assembly.

Cylinder Safety Valves Pop Frequently

On some engines, a cylinder relief (safety valve) is provided for each cylinder. The function of the valve is to open when the cylinder pressures exceed a safe operating limit. The valve opens or closes a passage leading from the combustion chamber to the outside of the cylinder. The valve face is held against the valve seat by spring pressure. Tension on the spring is varied with an adjusting nut, which is locked when the desired setting is attained. The desired setting varies with the type of engine and may be found by referring to the manufacturer's technical manual.

Cylinder relief valves should be set at the specified lifting pressure. Continual lifting (popping) of the valves indicates excessive cylinder pressure of malfunction of the valves, either of which should be corrected immediately. Repeated lifting of a relief valve indicates that the engine is being overloaded, the load is being applied improperly, or the engine is too cold. Also, repeated lifting may indicate that the valve spring has become weakened, ignition or fuel injection is occurring too early, the injector is sticking and leaking, too much fuel is being supplied, or, in air injection engines, that the spray valve air pressure is too high. When frequent popping occurs, the engine must be stopped to determine and remedy the cause of the trouble. In an emergency, the fuel supply may be cut off in the affected cylinder. Relief valves must never be locked closed, except in an emergency. When emergency measures are taken, the valves must be repaired or replaced, as necessary, as soon as possible.

When excessive fuel is the cause of frequent safety valve lifting, the trouble may be due to the improper functioning of a high-pressure injection pump, a leaky nozzle or spray valve, or a loose fuel cam (if adjustable); or, in some systems such as the common rail, the fuel pressure may be too high.

A safety valve that is not operating properly should be removed, disassembled, cleaned and inspected. Check the valve and valve seat for pitting and excessive wear and the valve spring for possible defective conditions. When a safety valve is removed for any reason, the spring tension must be reset. This procedure varies to some extent, dependent on the valve construction.

Except in emergencies, it is advisable to shut an engine down when troubles cause safety valve popping.

Clogged or partially obstructed exhaust ports may also cause the cylinder safety valve to lift. This condition will be of infrequent occurrence if proper planned maintenance procedures are followed. If it does occur, the resulting increase in cylinder pressure may be sufficient to cause safety valve popping. Clogged

Table   1.—Symptoms of engine trouble

| NOISES | INSTRUMENT INDICATIONS | | | SMOKE | CONTAMINATION OF LUBE OIL, FUEL, OR WATER |
	PRESSURE	TEMPERATURE	SPEED		
POUNDING (MECHANICAL)	LOW LUBE OIL PRESSURE	LOW LUBE OIL TEMPERATURE	IDLING SPEED NOT NORMAL	BLACK EXHAUST SMOKE	FUEL OIL IN THE LUBE OIL
	HIGH LUBE OIL PRESSURE	HIGH LUBE OIL TEMPERATURE	MAXIMUM SPEED NOT NORMAL	BLUISH-WHITE EXHAUST SMOKE	WATER IN THE LUBE OIL
KNOCKING (DETONATION)	LOW FUEL OIL PRESSURE (IN LOW-PRESSURE FUEL SUPPLY SYSTEM)	LOW COOLING WATER TEMPERATURE (FRESH)		SMOKE ARISING FROM CRANKCASE	OIL OR GREASE IN THE WATER
CLICKING (METALLIC)	LOW COOLING WATER PRESSURE (FRESH)	HIGH COOLING WATER TEMPERATURE (FRESH)		SMOKE ARISING FROM CYLINDER HEAD	WATER IN THE FUEL OIL
					AIR OR GAS IN THE WATER
	LOW COOLING WATER PRESSURE (SALT)	LOW CYLINDER EXHAUST TEMPERATURE		SMOKE FROM ENGINE AUXILIARY EQUIPMENT (BLOWERS, PUMPS, ETC.)	METAL PARTICLES IN LUBE OIL
RATTLING	HIGH COOLING WATER PRESSURE (SALT)	HIGH EXHAUST TEMPERATURE IN ONE CYLINDER			
	LOW COMPRESSION PRESSURE				
	LOW FIRING PRESSURE				
	HIGH FIRING PRESSURE				
	LOW SCAVENGING AIR RECEIVER PRESSURE (SUPERCHARGE ENGINE)				
	HIGH EXHAUST BACK PRESSURE				

exhaust ports will also cause overheating of the engine, high exhaust temperatures, and sluggish engine operation.

Clogging of cylinder ports can be avoided by removing carbon deposits at prescribed intervals. Some engine manufacturers make special tools for port cleaning. Round wire brushes of the proper size are satisfactory for this work. Care must be taken in cleaning cylinder ports to prevent carbon's entering the cylinder—the engine should be barred to such a position that the piston blocks the port.

VIII. SYMPTOMS OF ENGINE TROUBLE

In learning to recognize the symptoms that may help you locate the causes of engine trouble, you will find that experience is the best teacher. Even though written instructions are essential for efficient troubleshooting, the information usually given serves only as a guide. It is very difficult to describe the sensation that you should feel when checking the temperature of a bearing by hand; the specific color of exhaust smoke when pistons and rings are worn excessively; and, for some engines, the sound that you will hear if the crankshaft counterweights come loose. You must actually work with the equipment in order to associate a particular symptom with a particular trouble. Written information, however, can save you a great deal of time and eliminate much unnecessary work. Written instructions will make detection of troubles much easier in practical situations.

Symptoms which indicate that a trouble exists may be in the form of an unusual noise or instrument indication, smoke, or excessive consumption or contamination of the lube oil, fuel, or water. Table 1 is a general listing of various trouble symptoms which the operator of an engine may encounter.

NOISES

The unusual noises which may indicate that a trouble exists or is impending may be classified as pounding, knocking, clicking, and rattling. Each type of noise must be associated with certain engine parts or systems which might be the source of trouble.

Pounding is a mechanical knock or hammering (not to be confused with a fuel knock). It may be caused by a loose, excessively worn, or broken engine part. Generally, troubles of this nature will require major repairs.

Detonation (knocking) is caused by the presence of fuel or lubricating oil in the air charge of the cylinders during the compression stroke. Excessive pressures accompany detonation. If detonation is occurring in one or more cylinders, an engine should be stopped immediately to prevent possible damage.

Clicking noises are generally associated with an improperly functioning valve mechanism or timing gear. If the cylinder or valve mechanism is the source of metallic clicking, the trouble may be due to a loose valve stem and guide, insufficient or excessive valve tappet clearances, a loose cam follower or guide, broken valve springs, or a valve that is stuck open. A clicking in the timing gear usually indicates that there are some damaged or broken gear teeth.

Rattling noises are generally due to vibration of loose engine parts. However, an improperly functioning vibration damper, a failed antifriction bearing, or a gear-type pump operating without prime are also possible sources of trouble when rattling noises occur.

When you hear a noise, first make sure that it is a trouble symptom. Each diesel engine has a characteristic noise at any specific speed and load. The noise will change with a change in speed or load. As an operator you must become familiar with the normal sounds of an engine. Abnormal sounds must be investigated promptly. Knocks which indicate a trouble may be detected and located by special instruments or by the use of a "sounding bar" such as a solid iron screwdriver or bar.

INSTRUMENT INDICATIONS

An engine operator probably relies on the instruments to warn him of impending troubles more than on all the other trouble symptoms combined. Regardless of the type instrument being used, the indications are of no value if inaccuracies exist. Be sure an instrument is accurate and operating properly. All instruments must be tested at specified intervals, or whenever they are suspected of being inaccurate.

SMOKE

The presence of smoke can be quite useful as an aid in locating some types of trouble, especially if used in conjunction with other trouble symptoms. The color of exhaust smoke also can be used as a guide in troubleshooting.

The color of engine exhaust is a good, general indication of engine performance. The exhaust of an efficiently operating engine has little or no color. A dark, smoky exhaust indicates incomplete combustion; and the darker the color, the greater the amount of unburned fuel in the exhaust. Incomplete combustion may be due to a number of troubles. Some manufacturers associate a particular type of trouble with the color of the exhaust. The more serious troubles are generally identified with either black or bluish-white exhaust colors.

EXCESSIVE CONSUMPTION OF LUBE OIL, FUEL, OR WATER

An operator should be aware of engine trouble whenever excessive consumption of any of the essential liquids occurs. The possible troubles signified by excessive consumption will depend on the system in question; leakage, however, is one trouble which may be common to all. Before starting any disassembly, check for leaks in the system in which excessive consumption occurs.

ANSWER SHEET

TEST NO. _____ PART _____ TITLE OF POSITION _____
(AS GIVEN IN EXAMINATION ANNOUNCEMENT - INCLUDE OPTION, IF ANY)

PLACE OF EXAMINATION _____ DATE _____
(CITY OR TOWN)   (STATE)

RATING

USE THE SPECIAL PENCIL.   MAKE GLOSSY BLACK MARKS.

	A B C D E		A B C D E		A B C D E		A B C D E		A B C D E
1	‖ ‖ ‖ ‖ ‖	26	‖ ‖ ‖ ‖ ‖	51	‖ ‖ ‖ ‖ ‖	76	‖ ‖ ‖ ‖ ‖	101	‖ ‖ ‖ ‖ ‖
2	‖ ‖ ‖ ‖ ‖	27	‖ ‖ ‖ ‖ ‖	52	‖ ‖ ‖ ‖ ‖	77	‖ ‖ ‖ ‖ ‖	102	‖ ‖ ‖ ‖ ‖
3	‖ ‖ ‖ ‖ ‖	28	‖ ‖ ‖ ‖ ‖	53	‖ ‖ ‖ ‖ ‖	78	‖ ‖ ‖ ‖ ‖	103	‖ ‖ ‖ ‖ ‖
4	‖ ‖ ‖ ‖ ‖	29	‖ ‖ ‖ ‖ ‖	54	‖ ‖ ‖ ‖ ‖	79	‖ ‖ ‖ ‖ ‖	104	‖ ‖ ‖ ‖ ‖
5	‖ ‖ ‖ ‖ ‖	30	‖ ‖ ‖ ‖ ‖	55	‖ ‖ ‖ ‖ ‖	80	‖ ‖ ‖ ‖ ‖	105	‖ ‖ ‖ ‖ ‖
6	‖ ‖ ‖ ‖ ‖	31	‖ ‖ ‖ ‖ ‖	56	‖ ‖ ‖ ‖ ‖	81	‖ ‖ ‖ ‖ ‖	106	‖ ‖ ‖ ‖ ‖
7	‖ ‖ ‖ ‖ ‖	32	‖ ‖ ‖ ‖ ‖	57	‖ ‖ ‖ ‖ ‖	82	‖ ‖ ‖ ‖ ‖	107	‖ ‖ ‖ ‖ ‖
8	‖ ‖ ‖ ‖ ‖	33	‖ ‖ ‖ ‖ ‖	58	‖ ‖ ‖ ‖ ‖	83	‖ ‖ ‖ ‖ ‖	108	‖ ‖ ‖ ‖ ‖
9	‖ ‖ ‖ ‖ ‖	34	‖ ‖ ‖ ‖ ‖	59	‖ ‖ ‖ ‖ ‖	84	‖ ‖ ‖ ‖ ‖	109	‖ ‖ ‖ ‖ ‖
10	‖ ‖ ‖ ‖ ‖	35	‖ ‖ ‖ ‖ ‖	60	‖ ‖ ‖ ‖ ‖	85	‖ ‖ ‖ ‖ ‖	110	‖ ‖ ‖ ‖ ‖

Make only ONE mark for each answer.   Additional and stray marks may be counted as mistakes.   In making corrections, erase errors COMPLETELY.

	A B C D E		A B C D E		A B C D E		A B C D E		A B C D E
11	‖ ‖ ‖ ‖ ‖	36	‖ ‖ ‖ ‖ ‖	61	‖ ‖ ‖ ‖ ‖	86	‖ ‖ ‖ ‖ ‖	111	‖ ‖ ‖ ‖ ‖
12	‖ ‖ ‖ ‖ ‖	37	‖ ‖ ‖ ‖ ‖	62	‖ ‖ ‖ ‖ ‖	87	‖ ‖ ‖ ‖ ‖	112	‖ ‖ ‖ ‖ ‖
13	‖ ‖ ‖ ‖ ‖	38	‖ ‖ ‖ ‖ ‖	63	‖ ‖ ‖ ‖ ‖	88	‖ ‖ ‖ ‖ ‖	113	‖ ‖ ‖ ‖ ‖
14	‖ ‖ ‖ ‖ ‖	39	‖ ‖ ‖ ‖ ‖	64	‖ ‖ ‖ ‖ ‖	89	‖ ‖ ‖ ‖ ‖	114	‖ ‖ ‖ ‖ ‖
15	‖ ‖ ‖ ‖ ‖	40	‖ ‖ ‖ ‖ ‖	65	‖ ‖ ‖ ‖ ‖	90	‖ ‖ ‖ ‖ ‖	115	‖ ‖ ‖ ‖ ‖
16	‖ ‖ ‖ ‖ ‖	41	‖ ‖ ‖ ‖ ‖	66	‖ ‖ ‖ ‖ ‖	91	‖ ‖ ‖ ‖ ‖	116	‖ ‖ ‖ ‖ ‖
17	‖ ‖ ‖ ‖ ‖	42	‖ ‖ ‖ ‖ ‖	67	‖ ‖ ‖ ‖ ‖	92	‖ ‖ ‖ ‖ ‖	117	‖ ‖ ‖ ‖ ‖
18	‖ ‖ ‖ ‖ ‖	43	‖ ‖ ‖ ‖ ‖	68	‖ ‖ ‖ ‖ ‖	93	‖ ‖ ‖ ‖ ‖	118	‖ ‖ ‖ ‖ ‖
19	‖ ‖ ‖ ‖ ‖	44	‖ ‖ ‖ ‖ ‖	69	‖ ‖ ‖ ‖ ‖	94	‖ ‖ ‖ ‖ ‖	119	‖ ‖ ‖ ‖ ‖
20	‖ ‖ ‖ ‖ ‖	45	‖ ‖ ‖ ‖ ‖	70	‖ ‖ ‖ ‖ ‖	95	‖ ‖ ‖ ‖ ‖	120	‖ ‖ ‖ ‖ ‖
21	‖ ‖ ‖ ‖ ‖	46	‖ ‖ ‖ ‖ ‖	71	‖ ‖ ‖ ‖ ‖	96	‖ ‖ ‖ ‖ ‖	121	‖ ‖ ‖ ‖ ‖
22	‖ ‖ ‖ ‖ ‖	47	‖ ‖ ‖ ‖ ‖	72	‖ ‖ ‖ ‖ ‖	97	‖ ‖ ‖ ‖ ‖	122	‖ ‖ ‖ ‖ ‖
23	‖ ‖ ‖ ‖ ‖	48	‖ ‖ ‖ ‖ ‖	73	‖ ‖ ‖ ‖ ‖	98	‖ ‖ ‖ ‖ ‖	123	‖ ‖ ‖ ‖ ‖
24	‖ ‖ ‖ ‖ ‖	49	‖ ‖ ‖ ‖ ‖	74	‖ ‖ ‖ ‖ ‖	99	‖ ‖ ‖ ‖ ‖	124	‖ ‖ ‖ ‖ ‖
25	‖ ‖ ‖ ‖ ‖	50	‖ ‖ ‖ ‖ ‖	75	‖ ‖ ‖ ‖ ‖	100	‖ ‖ ‖ ‖ ‖	125	‖ ‖ ‖ ‖ ‖

ANSWER SHEET

TEST NO. ____________ PART ______ TITLE OF POSITION ______________________________
(AS GIVEN IN EXAMINATION ANNOUNCEMENT - INCLUDE OPTION, IF ANY)

PLACE OF EXAMINATION ______________________________ (CITY OR TOWN) ______ (STATE) DATE ______________

RATING

USE THE SPECIAL PENCIL. MAKE GLOSSY BLACK MARKS.

1 A B C D E	26 A B C D E	51 A B C D E	76 A B C D E	101 A B C D E
2 A B C D E	27 A B C D E	52 A B C D E	77 A B C D E	102 A B C D E
3 A B C D E	28 A B C D E	53 A B C D E	78 A B C D E	103 A B C D E
4 A B C D E	29 A B C D E	54 A B C D E	79 A B C D E	104 A B C D E
5 A B C D E	30 A B C D E	55 A B C D E	80 A B C D E	105 A B C D E
6 A B C D E	31 A B C D E	56 A B C D E	81 A B C D E	106 A B C D E
7 A B C D E	32 A B C D E	57 A B C D E	82 A B C D E	107 A B C D E
8 A B C D E	33 A B C D E	58 A B C D E	83 A B C D E	108 A B C D E
9 A B C D E	34 A B C D E	59 A B C D E	84 A B C D E	109 A B C D E
10 A B C D E	35 A B C D E	60 A B C D E	85 A B C D E	110 A B C D E

Make only ONE mark for each answer. Additional and stray marks may be counted as mistakes. In making corrections, erase errors COMPLETELY.

11 A B C D E	36 A B C D E	61 A B C D E	86 A B C D E	111 A B C D E
12 A B C D E	37 A B C D E	62 A B C D E	87 A B C D E	112 A B C D E
13 A B C D E	38 A B C D E	63 A B C D E	88 A B C D E	113 A B C D E
14 A B C D E	39 A B C D E	64 A B C D E	89 A B C D E	114 A B C D E
15 A B C D E	40 A B C D E	65 A B C D E	90 A B C D E	115 A B C D E
16 A B C D E	41 A B C D E	66 A B C D E	91 A B C D E	116 A B C D E
17 A B C D E	42 A B C D E	67 A B C D E	92 A B C D E	117 A B C D E
18 A B C D E	43 A B C D E	68 A B C D E	93 A B C D E	118 A B C D E
19 A B C D E	44 A B C D E	69 A B C D E	94 A B C D E	119 A B C D E
20 A B C D E	45 A B C D E	70 A B C D E	95 A B C D E	120 A B C D E
21 A B C D E	46 A B C D E	71 A B C D E	96 A B C D E	121 A B C D E
22 A B C D E	47 A B C D E	72 A B C D E	97 A B C D E	122 A B C D E
23 A B C D E	48 A B C D E	73 A B C D E	98 A B C D E	123 A B C D E
24 A B C D E	49 A B C D E	74 A B C D E	99 A B C D E	124 A B C D E
25 A B C D E	50 A B C D E	75 A B C D E	100 A B C D E	125 A B C D E